How to Be a Missionary in Your Hometown

About the author: Joel Nagel has led the Lansing Area Church of Christ in Lansing, Michigan since 2002. He studied history at Michigan State University where he focused on building a Christian campus ministry. While advancing the gospel and spending time with his family, Joel also loves trail running and exploring waterfalls in Michigan's Upper Peninsula. He and his wife, Beth, have two daughters.

Contents

Introduction 6

    Missionary Events Planner 13

    Mission Map 14

    Mission Moments 15

Section 1: Heart

Week 1: The Heart of God 19

    Prayer Banner 36

Week 2: The Place of Prayer 39

Week 3: The Power of the Gospel 57

    Gospel Vision Chart 75

Week 4: The Presence of Jesus 77

Section 2: Feet

Week 5: Heroes of the Faith—Old Testament 99

Week 6: The Art of Hospitality 115

Week 7: Heroes of the Faith—New Testament 133

Week 8: The Word of Life 149

Section 3: Hands

Week 9: The Least of These 167

Week 10: The Harvest is Plentiful 181

Week 11: The Workers Are Few 199

Week 12: The Celebration of the Saints 217

    Epilogue 224

    Appendix A: Old School Bible Study Series 225

    Appendix B: Bible Talk Starter Pack 237

    Appendix C: Soul Talk: How is Your Soul Doing? 242

Dedication

To Dad and Mom,
for sharing your faith with me.

Thank you Lezlee Worthington for
making this book beautiful with your linocut prints.

Introduction

"And they took offense at him. But Jesus said to them, 'A prophet is not without honor except in his own town and in his own home.'"

—Matthew 13:57

"Jesus is Lord!"

When I said those words at the waters of baptism, I was 14 years old. Our fellowship of churches was sending people to every corner of the world on mission teams. I'm sure I loved Jesus, but I'm also certain that I loved the dream of being a radical overseas missionary who planted a church in a jungle or on top of a mountain or whatever exotic place God would take me. I came out of the water wanting to live life on the edge in some faraway place that needed Jesus.

I was raised on stories of disciples of Jesus going anywhere, doing anything, and giving up everything. I knew people who had taken the "One Suitcase Challenge" to begin ministry work in India. I even got a taste of mission work through *HOPE Youth Corps* trips each summer. I remember being sincerely worried as a teenager that I would not get to go overseas because our fellowship would finish evangelizing the world before I was old enough to plant a church.

I went to Michigan State University (Go Green!) and joined a small satellite ministry of the church I had grown up in. When I graduated in 2001, I was leading the ministry in Lansing, Michigan and I have been leading this church, in this place, EVER SINCE. I haven't travelled much. I haven't moved a bunch of times. I've just been here leading this church and watching God make it grow.

I probably don't need to tell you that Lansing, Michigan is one of the least exotic places on the planet Earth. Perhaps the best word to describe my city would be "regular." The most exciting happenings are that we finally got a Costco and one of our restaurants was featured on *"Diners, Drive Ins, and Dives"*.

How boring! I know introductions are supposed to be exciting enough to hook the reader on the book. But that's my whole point I guess. *Boring and regular are not the enemies of radical and faithful. You don't need a passport to do great things for God, you just need to believe that...*

Jesus is Lord

That pledge of a good conscience doesn't get nullified because Jesus didn't lead me the way I dreamed that he would. *Sure, the world needs missionaries. I still marvel at those who continue to sacrifice and move overseas to save souls by the power of God.* But the lost world isn't just over there—it's right here—wherever you're reading this book. And following Jesus in a radical way isn't place specific. Jesus is Lord in the Middle East and the Midwest. People are just as lost in South Korea as they are in South Carolina.

When Jesus went to his hometown, he was rejected. His mission in Nazareth ran up against an extreme lack of faith and he could do no miracles there. Your town and your church may be experiencing the same lack of faith and lack of miracles—but for the exact opposite reason. In Nazareth, the people didn't believe in the mission of Jesus. In your town, it may be that you do not believe in the mission of Jesus. Over the next 12 weeks we're going to change that.

The Mission of Jesus

The heart of a disciple is to imitate Jesus. So what does Jesus teach us about being on the mission?

> *Throughout this book you will need to read a lot of Bible verses. Please don't skip any of the readings! Go ahead and get your Bible out and get started now by reading Luke 10:1-9 before reading on.*

Scholars refer to these verses in Luke as the "missional discourse". This is Jesus telling the 72 *how* to go and make disciples. Jesus' instructions to his disciples were widespread even before the gospels were written and distributed (see 1 Corinthians 9:14 which was written before any of the gospels). These words aren't just a life hack or friendly tips on how to be more effective at evangelism. They are how we are to go about the mission. They are instructions from the Lord himself to missionaries.

Speaking of instructions, I used to go full rage monster when putting together furniture from Ikea or anything with detailed instructions. But the last time I put something together (a loft for my daughter), I had no frustration because I went into it resigned to the fact that at some point I'd miss a direction even though I was paying careful attention. Before I even started, I assumed I'd have to take apart some of what I built and rebuild it correctly. I see these instructions from Jesus the same way. I have read them and preached them many times and yet I keep missing important details. Even now as I write a book on the mission, I'm resigned to the fact that I'm still missing something and I'll have to tear some things apart and restart. Let's try our best anyway to break these instructions down and not to miss any important details.

Jesus sends the 72 out in pairs with the goal of finding laborers—not just saving souls. He wants his disciples to pray that they will find new disciples who will make more disciples. He wants them to depend on God so they aren't allowed to take anything with them (it's a NO suitcase challenge!).

> *And this is how they are to make disciples of Jesus who make more disciples of Jesus: They are to find a household that is open to the good news of Jesus and they are to STAY THERE.*

Finding a place and staying there was so important that if the disciples (who brought nothing with them) wanted to eat and have shelter they needed to find a home to remain in. Even as more people and households opened up to the gospel in that town they weren't even supposed to go to another house in that town. They were instructed to heal the sick and preach the gospel right where they were.

Some historical context and a little imagination can help us understand the wisdom of Jesus' missionary instructions. Jesus isn't just helping his disciples to be evangelistic—he's establishing his kingdom. There are no churches or church buildings. There are Christian households. In Capernaum, where Peter and John lived, Jesus had turned Peter's household into the first church in Galilee (Luke 4:38-41), from which he healed the sick and preached the gospel. His work there went way beyond saving a few fishermen. Jesus established a homebase for the gospel to spread in that city by spending time with a family and showing them the power and love of Christ. The Twelve (Luke 9:1-6) and the seventy-two who were to go and do the same thing Jesus had already done in Capernaum in all the towns and villages of Galilee.

What was the result? In all the places where Jesus was about to go, there was a home-base for the gospel; a household, a house church, that could continue to save souls in that place long after Jesus' physical presence was gone. That's an amazing plan!

When we attempt to personally apply the missional discourse we should ask ourselves who we are and what we are supposed to be doing. We aren't Jesus (more on that later in the book), we aren't the 12 or even the 72. We are the people in the house/apartment/dorm that welcomed a disciple who prepared our hearts to meet Jesus and we responded to the gospel with saving faith.

> *We are the ones left right where we are on purpose to be a home-base for the gospel in our town or village or city; to heal the sick and preach the gospel, so every heart could be made ready for Jesus when he comes again.*

Maybe, like me, you also dreamed of being a missionary one day. Or maybe the idea of living in a foreign land and preaching the gospel is the last thing you'd ever want to do. Either way, if you made Jesus Lord, then you have been chosen to be a missionary in your hometown. When I say hometown, I don't mean where you are from—I mean the place where you live and work and play right now—your home. You are a home-base for the saturation of the gospel of Jesus Christ. No passport, no visa, no u-haul, no airplanes required; just a disciple of Jesus on the mission of Jesus.

How to Be a Missionary in your Hometown

It's one thing to know that we are supposed to be hometown missionaries. It's a whole other thing to become one. This book has been created to train individuals and churches to become home bases for the spread of the good news about Jesus Christ. Consider this a 12 week crash course for disciples who want to make disciples, a.k.a. the only kind of disciple there is! This is so much more than a book. This is a training manual full of lessons, activities and challenges for you to complete. Don't just read it! **Do it.** The training is laid out with a main lesson (to be read on Sunday if possible) and then devotionals that will challenge your heart Monday through Saturday. *It is best to read each day and not skip ahead and if possible not fall behind.*

At the beginning of any class there is an orientation so you have some idea of what you are getting yourself into and to help you be successful. Here's what to expect over the next 3 months:

There are 3 sections. **Heart** is the first section where we will look at the heart behind making disciples. Doing the right thing for the wrong reasons or in the wrong way is always wrong. So we will begin this focus on sharing our faith by *not sharing our faith at all for the first three weeks.* You need to have a faith to share before you can share your faith! So we'll build our faith on a solid foundation first. Section 2 is called **Feet** because you'll be using your feet to take the gospel to places all over your city in creative, challenging and fun ways. Section 3 is called **Hands** because we'll end by looking at what it means to truly care for people as disciples and not just gain converts for the sake of numerical growth. Each week begins with a lesson that illustrates the main idea of the week. That lesson is followed up by smaller daily lessons to make you R.E.A.D.Y.

Are You R. E. A. D. Y.?

Because *How To Be A Missionary In Your Hometown* is a 12 week training program, each week is accompanied by daily training to make us ready for the mission. Paul makes a bold claim about the power of scripture when we put it into action in our lives. *"All Scripture is breathed out by God and profitable for teaching, for reproof, for correction, and for training in righteousness, that the man of God may be competent, equipped for every good work"* (2 Timothy 3:16-17). So, the Bible is not to be read as any other book. When we read it properly, we are training ourselves to be competent and equipped for all kinds of goodness. God wants to make us ready to be hometown missionaries. Here's how we'll get **R.E.A.D.Y.**: Read, Examine, Apply, Do, Yield.

Read

Each day begins with a reading from scripture related to the theme of the week. Don't skip this even if it's the most familiar scripture in the Bible. **Read God's Word.** Pray before you read it for insight. Read it out loud if possible. The word of God is powerful—but only if we read it!

Examine

After each reading we dive deeper into the text to provide background and insight to the passage and tie it in with the main theme of the week. Feel free to take your own notes on things that impact you as you read.

Apply

The application section guides us to think about what the passage means for us today. This might be different for each reader. You will be prompted to think and pray about applying the passage to your life by answering a question or two.

Do

This is the fun part! *We're going to do one thing each day because of what we've read in God's Word.* These things you do by God's strength will become **Mission Moments** that you can place on the **Mission Map** at your church if you are doing this as part of a church wide event or the **Mission Map** you draw in this book (Week 1) if you are taking this journey on your own. Pray about this part, plan it out, modify it to make sense in your situation and go for it!

Yield

The word yield has a couple of meanings and both apply here. First of all, yield means to surrender to another. That's a great way to end time with God and go and do something with what you read. Yield to God. Pray for him to be in control and for something amazing to happen. There is a **prayer prompt** to get your prayer going and help you talk to God in a creative way each day based on what you've read.

Yield also means a return on an investment, like when a farmer yields crops from seeds planted. When we read, apply and act on God's word we can expect to yield a return. It might not be the way we expect but if we're looking we'll be able to see what God is doing in our lives and all around us. Before you start each day's training look back at the previous day's devotional and write down what God yielded in your life the day before.

Other Resources For Immersing Yourself in The Mission

This book is loaded with interactive resources and tools to give you more than enough to become a hometown missionary. Look for these helpful tools as you read and put the reading into action:

- Some challenges will take some planning ahead of time but just follow the **"Looking Ahead"** prompts and you'll have no problem being prepared.

- Throughout the book there are **hashtag suggestions** that will allow you to share your experience with people reading the book in other hometowns. There are also **family devotionals** and family activities so your whole family/household can jump into the mission.

- *The best way to experience this book is with your entire church or ministry.* This book is available at a great discount when purchased by churches in bulk. **HometownMissionary.com** has been designed as a companion website to the book for ministry leaders. There, ministry leaders will find specific week by week instructions and resources that will help them lead a successful three month focus for groups of any size. Sermons, links, ideas, calendars, Bible studies, printables and even access to a weekly conference call are all available for no cost. I want to make it as easy as possible for you to get your whole church on the mission of Jesus Christ.

• The **appendices** at the end of the book include an accessible Bible study series for helping people become Christ followers, four easy Bible Talks (Bible Discussion Series) and the script for a Soul Talk gathering at your church.

Lastly, to give you a big picture of what it's going to take to become a hometown missionary, I've included a Missionary Calendar with key events. Your family or your church may have to switch some dates but this should give you a good idea of the amazing places your heart, hands and feet are about to go with God. I know looking at this might seem overwhelming right now, but I believe you'll be amazed at what God can do in just a few months when we decide to be on the mission in each of our hometowns. Feel free to write the actual dates of your church's events in the margin if you are doing this book as a church. You might be tempted to go solo, but get as many people involved as you can. I'm not trying to sell more books—Jesus never sent his disciples alone!

See the next page for the planner.

Hometown Missionary Events Planner

Wk	Chapter	Event
-3		Give Out Books
-2		
-1		Place Mission Map in Front of Church, Mission Memos
1	The Heart of God	
2	The Place of Prayer	Personal Prayer Spot & Banner/Church Prayer Spot
3	The Power of the Gospel	
4	The Presence of Jesus	
5	The Heroes of Faith: Old Testament	
6	The Art of Hospitality	Hospitality Week
7	The Heroes of Faith: New Testament	
8	The Word of Life	Bible Talk Week
9	The Least of These	Serve a Vulnerable Population
10	The Harvest is Plentiful	Churchwide Gospel Night
11	The Workers are Few	All Night Prayer
12	The Celebration of the Saints	Party!

It's time to start your training. Turn the page and begin your journey into the mission field that is your hometown.

MISSION MAP

Draw a basic map of your town here

MISSION MOMENTS

Record your mission moments here and
place the corresponding number on the map.

1. Prayer Spot

2.

3.

4.

5.

6.

7.

8.

9.

10.

11.

12.

13.

14.

15.

16.

17.

18.

19.

20.

Section 1: Heart

"For no good tree bears bad fruit, nor again does a bad tree bear good fruit, for each tree is known by its own fruit. For figs are not gathered from thornbushes, nor are grapes picked from a bramble bush. The good person out of the good treasure of his heart produces good, and the evil person out of his evil treasure produces evil, for out of the abundance of the heart his mouth speaks."

—Luke 6:43-45

The same mistake gets made over and over again. We focus on the fruit when Jesus clearly tells us to focus on the heart. We focus on the right words to say when the right heart will overflow with the treasure of the gospel.

We're not going to make that mistake anymore.

We're going to start with the heart and let God grow good fruit. To accomplish this I want to put a challenge before you that seems to go against everything this book is about. Don't share your faith for the next three weeks.

Now, if the Spirit is yelling at you to tell someone about Jesus, please listen to the Spirit. But, as far as it is up to you, I'd like you to pause sharing your faith. This may sound like the easiest challenge you've ever received but when you hear about who God is and how much he loves you on the pages that follow, I believe you'll have to bite your tongue even if you haven't shared your faith in years!

Here's why I want you to hit the pause button on your evangelism: God cares about the quality of our fruit and the contents of our hearts more than the quantity of conversions. We need to hit reset and examine why we share our faith so that we can be sure we have a faith to share and not just a habit or religious regimen.

There are two ways this reset happens. First, God can hit the reset button for us. Paul describes this in 1 Corinthians 3:13 when he looks at how the church in Corinth grew in number but also in division, saying, *"each one's work will become manifest, for the Day will disclose it, because it will be revealed by fire..."*. When God hits the reset button there is exposure and fire. Whatever was built poorly (with the wrong heart) is torn down so that we can stand confidently before God on Judgement Day. Instead of God having to come in and test what we're building with fire, we can test ourselves with the help of God, his word and his people. This may still be painful if we're honest but it sure beats option one!

So we're going to start over in our evangelism. And we're going to start with the heart. And not just any heart, or even our own hearts, but the heart of God.

Week 1: The Heart of God

"This is my beloved..."

—Matthew 3:17

Instead of sharing our faith with others, we're going to let God share his faith with us. Are you ready to be reached out to by God?

Beloved

Let me start by telling you about God's beloved. How tender and beautiful to call the one you love beloved! God himself speaks from heaven twice in the book of Matthew. And both times, speaking to his son Jesus, he calls him, "Beloved".

At his baptism, *"This is my beloved Son, with whom I am well pleased"* (Matthew 3:17). And on the Mount of Transfiguration when Moses and Elijah came to comfort him before his death, *"This is my beloved son, with whom I am well pleased; listen to him"* (Matthew 17:5). Jesus is the beloved of God. He knew it too. He identified with the words Isaiah spoke centuries earlier, *"Behold, my servant whom I have chosen, my beloved with whom my soul is pleased"* (Matthew 12:18, Isaiah 42:1).

It makes sense that God would tenderly call Jesus his beloved. They had enjoyed an unbroken relationship from the very beginning. Before time itself or any of creation existed, the Father, the Son and the Spirit existed in an intimate, eternal, unbreakable bond of love. It is a fallacy to think that God created us because he was lonely and needed something to love. The union of the trinity was and is the perfect expression of love in which all relational needs are completely met.

What I'm saying is that Jesus has *always* been the beloved of God. John says it too:

> *"In the beginning was the Word, and the Word was with God, and the Word was God. He was in the beginning with God. All things were made through him, and without him was not anything made that was made."* —John 1:1-3

And the writer of Hebrews begins his great work by stating this same fact:

> *"Long ago, at many times and in many ways, God spoke to our fathers by the prophets, but in these last days he has spoken to us by his Son, whom he appointed the heir of all things, through whom he also created the world."* —Hebrews 1:1-2

Can you imagine what it must have been like for the Father and the Son in that time before time? Jesus looking at his father whom he would call "Abba" and the Father reveling in the presence of his beloved son.

We know that the beloved son did not stay in heaven with the Father. In God's perfect timing he came to us, present, as a man. Close your eyes and try to imagine a timeline of eternity. Looking back, you see no beginning, it goes on forever into the past. And looking forward, there is no end. It extends to forever. And right in the middle there's a blink, a speck, interrupting the flow of the timeline, signifying the moment when Jesus was here. He spent maybe 30 years living life, breathing air, experiencing the joy and sadness that is human existence. And in those 30 years—a blink in the timeline of eternity—Jesus was still the beloved of God. And God made sure that Jesus knew it by breaking into our world to call him his beloved at his baptism and on that mountain where he was transfigured. For just 30 years he lived on this earth as the beloved of God and his whole mission, he repeats it again and again in the gospel of John, was to glorify his Father. Put into eternal perspective, he had just a moment in which he could bring glory to God as the beloved in the flesh.

And then, having glorified God with his brief life, Jesus died on the cross. The beloved cried back to the heavens, to his Father who had cried out "beloved" to him, but there was no answer. We know that he arose on the third day. We know that after 40 days he went to heaven where he sits enthroned to this day as the beloved of God where he will remain for eternity.

That's who Jesus is, was and always will be, yesterday and today and forever: The Beloved of God.

Don't you just want to tell someone about that?! But you can't! We agreed not to share our faith, remember. Plus, if you told someone about the beloved of God, you'd miss out on telling them the rest of the story that gets even better! It's great to see the relationship between God and Jesus. But what we really need to understand is the relationship between God and humanity, between God and each of us.

Peter was an eyewitness on the mountain when the Father called his son, "Beloved". He recounts the moment in his own words in 2 Peter 1:16-18. And then later in the same letter he addresses the letter's recipients, saying, *"This is now the second letter that I am writing to you, beloved"* (2 Peter 3:1a). Did you catch that? The one who heard God call Jesus "beloved" is now calling the Christians beloved. This isn't just some anomaly or Peter's way of being nice.

The apostle John was also on that mountain. He writes, *"**Beloved**, we are God's children now..."* (1 John 3:2a). What? He calls us beloved? He says we are God's children? Yes! In fact, he calls the Christians beloved ten times in his 3 letters.

Could it be that we are also the beloved of God? It sounds too good to be true; impossible even! After all there are some major differences between our story and Jesus' story. First of all, he is perfect and we most certainly are not. Unlike Jesus, our lives on earth are marred and faded by all the sin we've committed and brokenness we've caused. And secondly, he is eternal while even the oldest among us has come into existence only very recently when placed on God's timeline.

So how could we be the beloved?

Look at our sinfulness first. Paul wrote to the Roman church about God's plan to save both Jew and Gentile by asking them to remember the prophet Hosea who proclaimed this to the unfaithful and immoral people of his day, *"Those who were not my people I will call 'my people,' and her who was not beloved I will call 'beloved.' And in the very place where it was said to them, 'You are not my people,' there they will be called 'sons of the living God'"* (Romans 9:25-26, Hosea 2:23, 1:10). There it is again! Beloved. This is more than just a kind way to address Christians in the letters of Peter and John. In Christ Jesus, in that moment when the heavens were silent and Abba did not answer his Beloved, we became the beloved, sons of the living God. Our sin was removed so we could shine with all the glory of Christ in this blink of a life.

Yet, my blink of life is at 38 years right now. Not too old (no matter what my kids say) but certainly not eternal like Jesus. How could I be beloved like Jesus who was loved from before the beginning of time?

> *Praise be to the God and Father of our Lord Jesus Christ, who has blessed us in the heavenly realms with every spiritual blessing in Christ. For he chose us in him before the creation of the world to be holy and blameless in his sight. In loved he predestined us for adoption to sonship through Jesus Christ, in accordance with his pleasure and will—to the praise of his glorious grace, which he has freely given us in the One he loves. In him we have redemption through his blood, the forgiveness of sins, in accordance with the riches of God's grace that he lavished on us. With all wisdom and understanding, he made known to us the mystery of his will according to his good pleasure, which he purposed in Christ, to be put into effect when the times reach their fulfillment—to bring unity to all things in heaven and on earth under Christ.* —Ephesians 1:3-10

God chose us in Jesus *before the foundation of the world.* We know that Jesus always existed as the beloved of God but do you understand what this passage means? Do you understand what it means that we were predestined for adoption as sons because of the Beloved? Don't get distracted by the word predestined or the idea of predestination, it's not the same as predetermination.

This is going to sound crazy but please meditate on this and let it sink in. This passage means that like Jesus, you've always existed. I can't exactly tell you how but in the mind of God, in his plan and his purpose for this world, since before the creation of the world he has been totally in love with you. Just like Jesus you have always been and will always be the beloved of God.

And so that timeline you imagined earlier isn't just the life of Christ. That's who you are. Think about where you are right now. You're in the blink of glory! This is your moment in between the eternal to shine for God!

Yesterday and Today and Forever. We've covered our yesterday: we've been the beloved before the beginning of time. We've covered our today: we've got this life to live but we all mess it up and fall short of the glory of God so God sent Jesus to show us how it's done and to die so we could still be beloved despite our sin. So what about forever? Isn't that what we care about the most. Are we going to live forever? Are we going to be beloved forever?

The answer is yes and here's why: Jesus decided to share his faith with you.

There's this moment recorded in each of the gospels where it became possible for us to become the beloved of God for the rest of forever. It's the moment when Jesus wrestled with God in prayer about sharing his faith with us or not.

You know the feeling you get when you are about to talk to someone about God? It could be a stranger you're going to invite to church or a family member you're going to ask to study the Bible; the feeling is the same. I've been leading a church for 15 years and I still feel a pit in my stomach, a dull pain in the gut accompanied by sharp doubts in my head when I'm about to share my faith. And I hate that this is the truth—sometimes the pain in my stomach and the doubt in my brain cause my lips to stick together and my faith to stay with me instead of being shared. Fear still causes me to fail to share my faith. I pray in the moment and still sometimes I fail to act in a way that could lead to a person's eternal salvation.

It was in a garden that this whole sin thing became a problem in the beginning. And at the very end, eternity is described as a garden where God is intimately present with his people once again. So of course this moment where our salvation hung in the balance happened in a garden, the Garden of Gethsemane. I went to Gethsemane a few years ago. There are these really old olive trees still there. My group was led in a devotional (thanks Rich and Tony!) and then we had time to go and pray. I have prayed on my knees in the Garden of Gethsemane! And I still fail to share my faith!

Gethsemane means "olive press." There were different kinds of tools used in first century agriculture for each crop. Wheat was threshed. A board loaded with rocks would be slid over the wheat to crack the head and release the grain. Then a winnowing fork would be used to throw the wheat and the chaff (the broken outer shell) into the air. The chaff would blow away in the wind leaving a pile of whole grain wheat. Grapes began their journey into wine using people's feet as the perfect tool. The grapes needed to be squeezed, but not so hard that the seeds would break which would add bitterness to the wine. So both wheat and grapes went through intense processes to become useful, but neither was crushed nor broken completely.

Then there was the olive press. A giant circular stone, placed in a groove and strapped to the back of a donkey. Around and around the stone would roll over and over again until the olives were completely crushed and every last drop of oil was extracted. Jesus didn't pray at the wheat threshing floor or the grape press. Gethsemane was the olive press. He wasn't gently squeezed. He was "crushed for our iniquities". Completely broken and smashed. Drained and emptied.

I think about that feeling I get when the Spirit prompts me to share my faith multiplied 8 billion times to the level of today's population on earth. Crushing. No wonder he had to pray three times for another way even as he submitted to the

Father's will.

I think about the times I've received persecution. Only a handful of all the times I have shared my faith has it even been negative. Someone threw food at me once. I got called a name. I found a ripped up invite card. That's the worst of it. Then I think about the persecution Jesus faced when he shared his faith with me. Devastating. Betrayed, beaten, flogged, misrepresented, mocked and nailed to two wooden beams on a hill so all could see.

> *How do I get to be the beloved of God? How can such a blessed eternity even be possible? Because when Jesus got that pit in his stomach and that fear of persecution and he prayed about whether he was going to share his faith, he did it.*

In the garden he decided he would share his faith with me and with you. And it killed him. The Beloved died so we could be beloved sons of God forever.

Can you keep that to yourself for a few weeks?

This week in our daily devotionals we'll take a deeper look at God's heart and our own. It's one thing to see Jesus as the Beloved of God, it's a whole other thing to see yourself as God's beloved—but here's the challenge of the week: *See everyone through the heart of God—see every person in your life as the beloved of God—because they are.* He's loved every soul from the depths of eternity and he will love everyone no matter where they choose to spend eternity. This life is so brief, but that's what makes it so special—this is the moment in eternity where you and the people all around you get to choose to love God back.

When I first saw that I was God's beloved and everyone in my life was too, it radically changed my marriage and my relationship with my kids. It affected the way I saw all of my relationships. I even saw strangers differently. I was so much more patient. And while I still need to be reminded about this—it's had a lasting impact on how I see the world. *If God loves every single person with an eternal love, no matter what—then I can be more loving.* If God wants all of his beloved to be his children for eternity, then I can share my faith and pray for people and figure out what they need so they can see how amazing God is.

The devotional times this week will take you on a journey into God's love. We aren't going to share our faith but you can if you want. Let's begin this journey with no agenda. This is not to grow the church or for humanistic reasons—but for God—so we need to sit on this and try to see the world through God's eyes.

There's one challenge this week that is similar to sharing your faith. Who knows how powerful it could be? Write yourself a love letter from God and if you want, you can post it on social media and see what God does with it.

A new sister, Erin, in our church wrote a love letter about our Wednesday night services (midweek) and it touched my heart and I'm sure it had an impact. Erin and her husband Corey and other people who are new to our church are great reminders of what we sometimes take for granted. It's inspiring to see fresh faith and to see people come to midweek or discipleship group and ask questions like, "What is this?" "How are these people so loving?" "How am I learning so much about God?" People in your life that you share God with will be blown away by what you have in your church. But don't take my word for it. Here's what our sister wrote:

"On Wednesday evenings we are lucky to be able to have midweek dinner and service at church. The kids go into their worship groups during service while Corey and I along with the other adults stay to worship and hear God's word. While my son was downstairs during Kid's Church they ate a yummy snack and this is what he chose to do with his alphabet *Cheez Its* before eating them:

"If you are looking for a church I HIGHLY recommend our church. We have never felt more at home. The people and the atmosphere are incredible. We look forward to church every Sunday morning and on Wednesdays and we attend great Bible studies with friends and an awesome discipleship group! We love growing in faith with each other, our children, and our brothers and sisters in Christ! Come hear his word. Come see how incredible your life will be with God in it!"

I guess what this 10-year-old made with Alphabet *Cheez Its* in Kid's Church sums up this whole first chapter: God is Super. And we've got this great family that God is building. And it's time to bring as many as possible to experience it. And it's not hard; all of God's beloved just need to be missionaries in their hometowns!

Week 1: In the Field Training

Peek at the Week

This week is all about trying to see people the way God sees people. That starts with seeing ourselves through God's eyes. The easiest person to be critical of is ourselves. At times, we beat ourselves up and devalue our self-worth every hour on the hour. We lament our faults and wonder how anyone can love us. Enter God. He knows our shortcomings more than we ever will and yet he's head over heels, madly in love with us, his beloved. Can you see yourself as God sees you and love who you are? This isn't just some self-help-feel-good message. The way we see ourselves affects the message we share about Jesus or if we even share it at all! Who is going to share about how much God loves them if they can't experience God's love because they are so down on themselves? Seeing ourselves through God's eyes is a prerequisite for the real challenge we face in week one.

So, here's this week's great challenge: We should see every living soul as God's beloved. This will change your life! Your family, your co-workers, fellow students, neighbors and even strangers are eternally loved by God. Can you start to see people like that this week? The devotionals will be daily reminders of God's heart that we may change our hearts to be more like his.

Activities:

This week is light on action and big on heart. How else will we get to the heart of God? The one exception is Friday:

Looking Ahead: Friday

Write a love letter to yourself from God's perspective. You can share it on social media—I think that our online friends might be blown away by seeing how much God loves you. If you choose to share it, you can use these hashtags so fellow hometown missionaries can be inspired by your letter #HometownMissionary #LoveLetterFromGod. Search these hashtags and be inspired by what others have written as they come to see themselves through God's eyes.

> Start your hometown missionary experience by letting your family know how much God loves them:

Gather:

- Have your family gather together with their Bibles

- Sing a Spiritual Song or Two
- Ask what your kids learned in kid's church and talk about what you learned at church.

Read:

- Ephesians 1:3-7 and explain what it means to be the Beloved of God and how God has loved us for eternity. Tell your family that they are not an accident, they are part of God's plan and he loves them so much.

Activity:

- Lay on your bellies facing each other. Have everyone think of ways that they love each person in the family and share with one another what is beloved about them.

Craft:

- Make a timeline of eternity—plain printer paper will work. Put your life on the line as a tiny speck. Talk about what you want to do to glorify God in this moment and what it will be like when we all glorify God when heaven comes down.

Pray!

Monday: God is Brokenhearted _____

Read

Genesis 3:8-21

Examine

This is the story of the fall of Adam and Eve and you and I. God's footsteps make a heavy sound when we rebel and separate ourselves from his holiness and presence. Sin is a curse that has set all of humanity against God.

Often we imagine that this must make God angry. Even as we read the curses meted out to Adam, Eve and the serpent we can read anger into the text. But could it be that God isn't so much angry but rather brokenhearted?

In his words to the serpent we have the first Messianic prophecy in the Bible. (Genesis 3:15) God has not abandoned people because of their sin. There's still a difference between the serpent and his offspring and the offspring (or seed) of Eve. Jesus comes, born of God and of woman, to ultimately defeat the serpent (but not before being mortally wounded himself), giving humanity the chance to become the offspring of God again. That means that immediately after the first sin ever, God was already planning to save his people from their sin. In fact, he had our salvation planned through his Son from the very beginning of eternity. That's how beloved we are!

This isn't just theological wisdom. God's love for his children, even as his heart is broken by their sin, is tangible. As they are removed from the garden, God personally makes them clothes so they can cover their newfound shame and nakedness.

Apply

How have you rebelled and broken God's heart?

In what ways has God been kind to you even in the midst of your sin?

Do

Pray to see the world through the eyes of a brokenhearted God today. Look at your classmates and co-workers as the beloved of God living in rebellion just as you often have been. Try to filter today's news and information through the same lens. **Imagine what God must feel as he looks at his children.**

Yield

Pray to see people, flaws and all, through the eyes of a loving God.

"Lord, help me to see people the way you see people…"

Tuesday: God is Jealous _____

Read

Exodus 20:1-6

Romans 12:11

Examine

The ten commandments are more than just a list of rules. They give us an insight into the very character and nature of God. Just as you can learn a lot about a person by their likes and dislikes, we can learn a lot about God from the things he prohibits. In this sense, the second commandment is particularly illuminating as God begins to describe his character as the rationale for the command against idolatry. Of course, God doesn't need to give us any reasons for his commandments but in this case he tells us that one of the reasons we should not worship carved images and false gods is because he is "a jealous God." God describes himself as jealous! What images does the word jealous bring to mind? Are they things you would usually associate with God?

This may cause us to wonder since jealousy for us is a sin (see the 10th commandment in verse 17). Is there a double standard going on here? No, and here's why: When we are jealous over "our neighbor's house or wife or worker" or car or anything that belongs to a person, we are coveting something that is not God. To deeply desire something that is just a thing is just another way of committing idolatry. Here's the difference with God's jealousy: When he is jealous for us it is because he wants us to have him, not an idol, not something from your neighbor's house—he wants you to stop missing out on him—your creator and savior. Thus God's jealousy is the only acceptable form of jealousy.

We can actually share in his jealousy and there's even a word for it. In the biblical languages, jealous and zealous are actually the same word. When a person feels jealous on behalf of God (think Phineas in Numbers 25:1-11) it is called zeal. When we are jealous, we want something that is not the best. When we are zealous, we share God's desire for people to have the very best: God himself. Ponder Romans 12:11 in light of this.

Apply

Think about the idols that people in your life are worshipping. Write some of them down being specific about what you see them worshipping that is not God.

How would people's lives change if they desired God first instead of things?

How could your zeal (putting God first) impact your family and friends?

Do

Now think about idols that have crept into your life. What makes you jealous or unhappy? Those emotions are often indicators of idol worship. **Choose one idol that you will stop worshipping today** and write down what the idol is and how you will chop it down (See 2 Chronicles 34:1-8 for inspiration).

Yield

Pray for God to destroy the idols in your life and in the lives of your friends. Be ready. It is often a painful process to remove entrenched gods.

"God, you are my only God…"

Wednesday: God is Faithful _____

Read
2 Timothy 2:11-13

Examine
The Bible only needs a few sentences to convict us. This trustworthy little poem is so encouraging and so challenging at the same time. We are getting ready to share our faith. In order to do that we must have a faith to share. If you're reading this, you probably have faith but there's a big difference between having faith and being faithful (literally full of faith). How can we share our faith when we often have so little? Even Jesus' disciples struggled with having little faith as he lovingly encouraged them to shoot for just a mustard seed sized faith!

This poem takes us on a spiritual journey and we get wrapped up in its pattern. We die (repent), we will live. We endure, we will reign. We deny, he will deny. We are faithless...and he will still be faithful! The pattern is suddenly broken when it comes to faith and the explanation is simple: "He cannot deny himself."

Do you struggle to believe God sometimes? Does a lack of faith keep you from sharing your faith? Amazingly, this poem tells us that we can share our faith regardless of how faithful we feel. Our faithfulness matters, but just not anywhere near as much as his faithfulness matters.

Think about this: God has never once struggled to be faithful! He's never wondered if he exists. He's never had a problem seeing the ways he's working in our lives and in the world. He's never once had a crisis of confidence. "If we are faithless, he remains faithful." We are saved by faith. The people all around us can be saved by faith. His faith. He never gives up on us or anyone in this world that he lovingly created. It doesn't depend on us. It depends on him. And he will always be faithful.

Apply
In what ways have you struggled to be faithful? Are you doubting God as you think about being a hometown missionary?

How has God proven himself to be faithful to you?

Do
Nothing. If God's faithfulness does not depend on our faithfulness, then you should be able to see God working even when you aren't. So, **just look for God's faithfulness all around you as you go about your day.**

Yield

Pray to become faithful (full of faith). Pray that you will have faith to share that is not governed by your emotions but simply relies on God. After all, that's what faithfulness is—reliance on God.

"God, I believe you…"

Thursday: God is Patient

Read

2 Peter 3:1-13

Examine

Ouch! That's a brutal passage, but it teaches us encouraging things about the heart of our God. Before we look at God's heart we are told what people's hearts will be like as the years go by without God returning for salvation and judgment. "They will say, 'Where is the promise?…All things are continuing as they were from the beginning of creation'" (v. 4). Peter was right. That is what many people today think and say about God. Indeed, they scoff at his return. This may be the attitude of many of the people that we will try to reach in the coming weeks. Some openly scoff while others would never say that God isn't coming back but their lives tell a different story. We may even be tempted to doubt the promise of God's return and creation's restoration ourselves.

"But do not overlook this one fact, beloved…". Peter calls us *beloved* and then he calls us to remember why God has yet to return. It's not because he's waiting for some big event or for all the genealogies to add up to the right day. It actually has nothing to do with time or events. It has to do with his character. God is patient. He's patient because he wants every soul to reach repentance.

I love to dream about what eternity with God will be like. I think the best day on this fallen earth won't even be comparable to one day in the presence of God. There are not words to describe the amazingness. And yet, here we are, day after day, living saved lives in a condemned world. Jesus has already won the victory. Our lives are sealed with God. So why the wait? What would be so important that God would delay eternity? The answer is every beloved person on this earth is that important.

Every day, when we wake up and Jesus hasn't returned, is a day that God has given to his beloved. He wants to be with us so badly, but he's patient, willing to wait, "that all should reach repentance." There is no day without a purpose. Every day is an opportunity to honor the heart of God and reach one more of his beloved.

Apply

Peter provides our application in this passage when he asks this in verse 11, *"Since all of these things are thus to be dissolved, what sort of people ought you to be in lives of holiness and godliness?"* So...what sort of person ought you be? What would you change if you saw the world through God's eyes and heart?

Do

Take on this characteristic of God and be radically patient. Be patient with your loved ones (often they are the ones we have the least patience for). Be patient with other drivers (don't pass the slow person—just be okay with being 1 minute later). And remember this isn't for you. A display of radical patience might just be the thing that turns someone from scoffing at God to seeing his love and reaching for repentance. Being patient shows the world a glimpse of what eternity with God will be like.

Yield

"Father, I will wait patiently..."

Friday: God is Love

Read

1 John 4:7-21

Examine

Just as Peter did in yesterday's passage, John addresses the recipients of his letter as beloved. There must be something about spending time with Jesus that makes a person feel so loved that they take on the identity of one who is loved—they self identify as beloved. And it follows that someone who knows how much they are loved finds it easier to love others. The best of us loves in fits and starts. But God *is* love. That means his very nature is love. Since God is incapable of being unloving, then everything he does is done in love.

So often our lives are filled with fear. Maybe when you first held this book about sharing your faith you were filled with fear. John puts before us that there is a connection between fear and love. We don't naturally think of love as the antidote of fear but we're told, *"there is no fear in love, but perfect love casts out fear."* When we consider the things we fear this makes perfect sense. We fear rejection. Love is the opposite of rejection. We fear being alone. When we are loved we never feel alone. We fear being misunderstood. Love completely understands. We fear embarrassment. How can we feel embarrassed in front of those who perfectly love us? We fear death. Love has even conquered death. All of those fears, without the remedy of perfect love, cause us to do things that lead to broken hearts and a broken world. We combat rejection by being people pleasers. We battle loneliness with sinful relationships. We accept quick fixes and comfortability when we could be receiving perfect love from God.

So much of the sin and brokenness of our world is caused by the fear of not being loved. We'll see this more clearly in a couple of weeks but the gospel is the ultimate answer to our fear of not being loved. On the cross, "the love of God was made manifest to us...that we may live" (v. 9).

Apply

What are you afraid of? Specifically, when it comes to sharing your faith, what scares you? Some common responses are rejection/persecution, a lack of knowledge or ability, developing a reputation as a "Bible thumper", the time and effort that it takes to help someone, and so on. Pray about and write down what scares you and then answer each fear with an aspect of God's love. Ultimately, there's nothing to fear as we share our faith because it's all up to God, anyway.

Do

Write a love letter from God to yourself as his beloved. Take into account all the things we've learned about the heart of God this week: God is brokenhearted, jealous, faithful, patient and love. If you'd like to inspire others who are training as hometown missionaries and share with people around you how much God loves you, post a picture of your letter using #HometownMissionary #LoveLetterFromGod. Need inspiration? Search those hashtags and see the ways God loves his beloved in other hometowns.

Yield

God, I'm afraid of...but you love me perfectly..."

Saturday: God is Counting on Us

Read
2 Corinthians 5:14-21

Examine

If you haven't written Friday's love letter from God please stop and take some time to write it now. We have to understand how much God loves us in Christ if we are to be controlled by Christ's love. The truth is he loved you enough to die for you. He knew you. He knew your faults and your rebellion and your brokenness and he loved you all the more up on that cross where he died. He arose, went to be with God, and sent us the Holy Spirit. The one perfect man died so we could live. His death saves us and it also gives us a purpose. Since he isn't physically here to tell people how much God loves them and that they can be saved from sin, he's counting on us to share this faith that has saved our souls.

That should amaze us beyond belief! All week we've been training in the nature of God. He is faithful and patient and loving while we struggle to live up to any of those characteristics! And yet the Master's plan is that we would be ambassadors for Christ, that we would have a ministry of reconciliation. And there's no backup plan if we fail. The next time we see Jesus it's all over and the new creation begins. He's not coming back to help us share our faith. And he doesn't need to because he's already given us his word, his Spirit and his body (the church).

You, beloved, are God's plan of salvation through Jesus Christ. To reconcile means to bring together two parties that are at odds. Right now many of your friends and family are at odds (or in outright rebellion) with God. You are the reconciler. Your ministry is to bring them to Jesus so he can fix their broken relationship with God. You are the ambassador, the representative of Jesus. The king can't physically be here. But that's okay because he's got you. Can you believe, beloved, that you are the plan?!

Apply

We talk about the importance of believing in God but what about how much God believes in us? He knows you and the people around you and he chose you, not them (not yet at least!). What an honor! God truly believes in you.

How does being chosen by God give you confidence for the mission ahead?

Why do you think God chose you? Go ahead and write down awesome things about yourself!

Do

Get ready for church tomorrow by thinking about the people and purpose of the church differently. These aren't your average people. The **people** in your church are the beloved of God that he has always loved and always will love. They are probably going through a lot of things right now in their lives but God loves them. **Think about that as you fellowship.** What an amazing honor it is to get together with the beloved of God and worship him!

Yet, there's more to this than a holy sing-a-long. One of the purposes of our worship is to start your week by remembering how you became the beloved of God. Jesus' love was poured out in blood and his body was broken to become the church. When we remember that together each week, it's not just so you can feel good. It's so you can do good. The whole rest of the week is before you and the vast majority of it will be spent not at church or even with church people. But if you go into Sunday morning with the right purpose, you'll enter the rest of your week ready to change the world around you.

Instead of going to church and then slowly becoming more worldly as the week drags on, do this: **Be the church** after you leave the worship service and make your world more holy because the beloved of God (you!) is walking in their midst.

Yield

God, you chose me...

My # Prayer Spot

The Lord's Prayer

Father...

Hallowed...

Your Kingdom Come

Give...

Forgive...

We Forgive...

Lead...

Prayer

Exodus
#Hometown

Your Kingdom Come

Three Big Prayers:
1.

2.

3.

How God Answered:
1.

2.

3.

Banner

17:8-16
Missionary

High Priestly Prayer
John 17

1. Jesus is awesome
   because:

2. Disciples—
   Supplication for
   Saints:

3. Those who will
   believe

Those who will believe

Pray For Me
1.

2.

3.

4.

Pray For Me
1.

2.

3.

4.

Week 2: The Place of Prayer

"And on the Sabbath day we went outside the city gate to the riverside, where we supposed there was a place of prayer, and we sat down..."
—Acts 16:13

In the Roman Empire, if there were not enough Jewish people in a city to build a synagogue, the Jews would gather by a river to worship on Sabbath. Philippi was a Roman garrison city and probably had very few Jewish people. Paul and his companions assumed that they would find other worshippers at the river and they were not wrong. Lydia was there and became the first-named convert on the continent of Europe; a continent that until recently was known as "The Christian Continent".

It all started at the place of prayer

I've always needed a special place to go and truly connect with God. When I was in college, I would spend many Saturday mornings riding my bike around campus looking for gardens, trails, parking garages or even cemeteries where I could be alone with God. About 10 years ago I discovered Burchfield Park. Its hundreds of acres of woods and miles of trails are where I love to pray. I walk among the trees and the birds and the Grand River and I talk out loud like a crazy person—except I know who I'm talking to and I know that he hears me. For years, I would drive 20 minutes a few times a week just to go there and pray. Recently, I got the chance to move to a house that borders the park. I get to live at my place of prayer!

There are two ways to think about the place of prayer. There's the physical place where we pray. We'll work on that in the daily devotionals this week.

> *There's also the place of prayer in our lives: the priority prayer takes and the value we place on being with God in prayer.*

By the end of this week, you'll have a physical place of prayer. By the end of this chapter I hope that your heart will understand the place that prayer should possess in your life.

In order to understand the place of prayer in your life, I want to help you understand one of the most difficult sections of the book of Revelation. I'll give you some context and then you can read the passage and come back to this chapter. I hope that as a side effect of reading this, Revelation will be less scary and more encouraging just as God intended it to be.

I approach Revelation through lenses. The first lens is context. As the last book of inspired scripture, God's last word, I'm convinced by what I've read in all that precedes Revelation that it wouldn't make sense to end the Bible with a weird, scary book of futuristic prophecy. God would never end his Word with a big question mark. But that's how many people approach revelation. The very word "revelation" means that God is revealing things to his people with this, his last book, not hiding them. So Revelation is not a question mark but rather an exclamation point! Furthermore, the original recipients of this letter are seven real life, flesh and blood churches in modern day Turkey who were beginning to endure a brutal persecution in which members of their churches were being arrested and even killed (Revelation 2:13). A book explaining the future threat of North Korea and the dangers of bar codes would NOT be encouraging. And encouragement is the biggest contextual lens we should focus on. Revelation was written to encourage hurting Christians near the end of the first century and because of its position as the last word in scripture it is meant to encourage hurting Christians throughout all centuries.

Revelation begins by describing Jesus in a jolting way. Even for Christians in the first century who knew people who walked with Jesus, there was a danger of Christianity becoming merely a religion. The linguistic style of Revelation stirs our hearts and minds out of complacency and causes us to think about Jesus in entirely new ways. As western thinkers, our minds are comfortable with abstract concepts so when we think about God we think about how he is loving or eternal or just. The Hebraic mind was less abstract. When they thought about the aspects of God, they thought in vivid pictures that pointed to greater truths. Where we might say God wants his churches to reflect his glory, Revelation says that the churches are lampstands. We then have to think about what that means: the churches aren't the light but they hold the light of Christ's glory and allow him to shine into the world. It's the same thing said in two very different ways. So in the first chapter, Jesus is described and the churches are introduced. In chapters 2-3, Jesus personally writes to each of the seven churches encouraging them to rely on him during the present hardship by reminding them who he is by using aspects of chapter 1 to personally relate to each church.

The letter to the last church is the most familiar to us for a couple of reasons. First, Jesus rebukes the church in Laodicea for being lukewarm and threatens to vomit them from his mouth. This is a brutal but also beloved passage for anyone who considers themselves a radical disciple of Jesus. Second, in Revelation 3:20 Jesus invites the Laodiceans to repent, saying, *"Behold, I stand at the door and knock. If anyone hears my voice and opens the door, I will come in to him and eat with him, and he with me."* Unfortunately, this passage is often falsely presented as an invitation for salvation by saying a prayer which is clearly not the context since it is written to a church of people that are already saved by the blood of Christ. That misinterpretation is even more tragic because it causes people to miss the significance of the very next thing that happens in Revelation.

"After this I looked, and behold, a door standing open in heaven!..."
—Revelation 4:1

I'm not sure if the Laodiceans ever repented and caught fire for God again but Revelation goes on to describe what would happen if they did. The door is open and we are transported to the throne room of God. From there, God rules the heavens and the earth and the symbols tell us this: 24 elders representing the patriarchs and the apostles, 4 living creatures representing the best of God's creation on earth. All of history and creation, day and night, worshipping God on the throne. What a picture!

In God's hand there is a scroll (5:1) written on the front and back and sealed with seven seals. When an ancient reader saw "scroll" he would have immediately thought "scripture". The Bible was not available at the Christian bookstore and it surely wasn't something you could read on your phone. At this point there wasn't even a New Testament and if you wanted to read the Old Testament, you had to go to the synagogue and unroll scrolls. So this scroll that God is holding in his hand is his word sealed with seven seals. A search is made in heaven and on earth and there is no one who can open up God's word. John writes, *"I began to weep loudly because no one was found worthy to open the scroll or look into it"* (5:4). John's reaction may seem strange to us, but it is how all of us should react once we understand what's going on. I know this chapter is about prayer and I promise we'll get there but first I want to show you something about evangelism that will change the way you pray forever.

The scroll is God's word and it is sealed up with no one able to open it. That means that the word of God is closed. It's not available to read, to pray through, to change lives, to give perspective, to teach, rebuke, correct or train ourselves. You can't share the gospel because it's sealed. If you can't share the gospel, then no one can believe it and be saved. Can you imagine if this was true? Knowing what you know about the power of God's word to save and to change the world, how would you feel if it was gone? Without his word we are truly alone and without purpose—we should "weep and weep".

> *The sad reality is that our lost friends and family live their lives as if God's word is sealed up and unavailable.*

They don't look at all that happens in the world and in their lives as part of the grand script that is the all encompassing word of God. They see a random, purposeless world and they probably try not to think about it to avoid depression. What a responsibility we've been given to show the word to the world!

Here's what happens next: The lion of Judah, a lamb looking as if it had been slain, is found worthy to open the scroll. Of course! The Word made flesh opens up the Word of God to us! The cross of Christ reveals that this life is not random; everything happens within His purpose and according to His will—even our salvation won by the lamb who was slain. An elder comforts John with this good news and all of heaven erupts again in worship. When things quiet down, the seals are broken one by one. God's word to mankind is revealed by Jesus himself! Don't you want to know what the Lamb of God reveals in his word? Then read it for yourself in Revelation 6:1-8:5 and I'll wait here for you to come back.

[Read Revelation 6:1-8:5]

How are you feeling after reading that? Confused? Discouraged? Maybe a little let down since I hyped it up so much and then it was all this stuff about the horsemen of the apocalypse and the 144,000? No matter how you are feeling, I promise you will be encouraged in just seven paragraphs and you'll see what all of this has to do with the place of prayer.

> *The word of God is more than just reading the Bible. Everything that happens in heaven and on earth is the word of God, the logos, the plan/script/promise. That is both scary and comforting.*

God has a plan and purpose and as faithful people we join in the prayer of the disciples and say, "Your kingdom come and your will be done on earth as it is in heaven." It encourages me that God's will is being accomplished even when it looks like everything on this planet is falling apart. But that also sobers me. When there are wars (the first rider/seal), or murders and mass killings (the second rider/seal), or famine, (the third rider/seal) all of those things happen within God's will and word. Maybe we will escape war, murder and famine, but none of us will escape the fourth rider and seal which is death, unless of course Jesus comes back first. I know this is not encouraging, but I asked you to give me seven paragraphs to get there and now we are one closer! Unfortunately, it's going to get worse before it gets better.

The fifth seal speaks to the uniquely tragic manner in which some Christians were experiencing death. They were dying as martyrs. Even this, the murder of Christians, takes place within the scroll that represents God's ultimate will. The readers of Revelation could be comforted by the image of the martyrs having a special place with God under the altar, signifying that their sacrifices were not in vain. But at the same time it must have been sobering for them and should certainly be sobering for us to hear God's response to their cries for him to come back and execute his righteous judgment on the world. God tells them to *"rest a little longer, until the number of their fellow servants and their brothers should be complete, who have been killed as they themselves had been"* (5:11).

Brutal! Can't we skip ahead to the encouraging part? We could, but then we wouldn't have the context for when disasters strike in our world. The sixth seal uses symbolic language to remind people immersed in the Old Testament of God's judgment. Disasters like hurricanes and earthquakes shake people's faith but God reveals that just like everything else, these are not random events, but are within the scope of his will. Perhaps the most challenging thing about these judgments (tests of faith) are that they affect Christians and non-Christians alike. A hurricane doesn't pick and choose its victims. The rain falls on the righteous and the unrighteous. Understanding this helps explain the pause of chapter 7 that takes place before the 7th seal is broken.

In the pause, the servants of Christ are sealed before disaster strikes. Obviously the 144,000, like all the numerology in Revelation is not to be taken literally. It's an exponential multiplication of 12 (tribes, disciples) that represents all of God's people. We're sealed. That should not be news to us. Of course, we're sealed with the Holy Spirit at our baptism (Acts 2:38). We've received this promised counselor that the world can't understand (John 14:16). He's the guarantee of our inheritance until we acquire possession of it (Ephesians 1:14). So, on the outside, when disaster strikes, when God judges (tests), it looks like everyone is suffering the same. But on the inside, those of us who've been sealed by the Spirit are experiencing something completely different even in the face of great hardship. The 144,000 from every tribe, people and language are worshipping all the way through! What feels like torture to those who don't see God is viewed as a faith-building test to the people who have God. The seal of the Spirit and the spiritual perspective he provides is the difference between a person being demolished by disaster or being a demonstration of God's power to save.

That's more encouraging, but it's still not the most encouraging thought. The first six seals teach us that Christians and non-Christians will all face suffering. It is not random. God's word and will are behind everything that happens in our world. Yet, as long as the wheat and the weeds grow together bad things will keep happening to good people. It's encouraging to know that God is in control but it also leaves us feeling helpless and small before the mighty and unfathomable will of God. Six seals and then the pause to talk about how we are sealed with the Holy Spirit. I think the pause is there before the seventh seal to build up the drama and anticipation for the seventh seal. In fact, I'm doing the same thing right now, making this paragraph a little longer because this is the 4th paragraph; the encouragement is about to come! (See how that works!)

Until this point in Revelation, heaven is a very noisy place. For a person who connects with God through quiet walks in the woods, I have to be honest that it doesn't really sound like the kind of place I'd like to spend eternity (good thing it's all symbolic). God's voice sounds like a rushing waterfall and a trumpet and thunder. There's always someone or something singing in a loud voice. Every so often all of heaven and earth sings all together, *"Holy, holy, holy."* The riders are yelling as they gallop on their horses. The martyrs are crying out, *"How long?"* The 144,000, all the people of God who ever lived are crying out with a loud voice, *"Salvation belongs to our God who sits on the throne, and the lamb!"* And then this:

> *"When the Lamb opened the seventh seal, there was silence in heaven for about half an hour. Then I saw the seven angels who stand before God, and seven trumpets were given to them. And another angel came and stood at the altar with a golden censer, and he was given much incense to offer with the prayers of all the saints on the golden altar before the throne, and the smoke of the incense, with the prayers of the saints, rose before God from the hand of the angel. Then the angel took the censer and filled it with fire from the altar and threw it on the earth, and there were peals of thunder, rumblings, flashes of lightning, and an earthquake."*   —Revelation 8:1-5

We've opened the seventh seal and we've reached the seventh paragraph. I hope you are ready to be encouraged. When we face the trials that God ordains as a part of human existence we are not without recourse. We are not helplessly adrift in the current of God's mighty will. We've been given access to the one writing the script by the blood of the lamb. The seventh seal tells us what happens when the saints pray to God. All the noise of heaven is silenced. The elders stop singing, the creatures cease their praises, the martyrs are hushed as prayer enters the throne room of God. The imagery of the altar, censer and smoke causes us to think about the temple and the priests who represented the people before God by sending their prayers up, mingled with the smoke of the burnt offering. Jesus always lives to intercede for us, to represent us before the throne of God when we pray.

> *When you pray everything in heaven stops to listen. God has never missed a prayer. He hears every whisper of his children, every detail of our hearts, every cry for help. He and all of heaven are tuned in.*

And he doesn't just listen to our prayers. He does something with them. He takes the requests of our hearts, a mere thought, a faith deficient whisper, a lonely cry. All the limping amens that make their way into the silenced throne room of God are thrown back to the earth as *"peals of thunder, rumblings, flashes of lightning and an earthquake."* My prayers go up as whispers in the woods and God sends them back down as thunder and lightning!

I encourage you to read on in Revelation for yourself but I'll summarize what happens next. Thunder and lightning answered prayer come in the form of angels blasting seven trumpets. Trumpets were used to warn people of disaster and to remind people to worship and even to blow down walls (Joshua 6-7). When we pray for people, God trumpets thunder and lightning in their lives in all of these ways. He warns them of disaster, often by giving them a little taste of disaster. He reminds them to worship, to seek him and find him. And he even tears down walls. We pray. God trumpets.

So you want to be a missionary in your hometown? You want to impact the lost and see souls saved? Who are you praying for? When the heavens are silenced, when God hushes the angel band, what names does he keep hearing before him? Who are you begging God to blast with his holy thunder? We can't tear down the walls that people build between themselves and God no matter how much effort we put in, but God can level the most fortified city with just one blast from his mouth. We're going to do this right. If you want to be a missionary in your hometown, you have to recognize that God saves souls and we do not. We have to recognize the place of prayer. It's the only place where we can have impact, where we can have a hand in the mission. If we don't pray for the people that we love then God isn't involved. We're going to get discouraged and frustrated and out of breath from blowing the trumpets that are reserved for the angels. This is the power and place of prayer—the preeminent weapon of the hometown missionary.

> *There's a spot right in the middle of a prayer banner that you'll be making this week—that's the door to the throne room of God!*

God needs to hear every single name again and again. His throne room should be littered with requests for the people in your town, at your work, in your family. This is why we still can't share our faith this week. We'd be working without God and we never want to do that. Here's what happens when we understand and practice the place of prayer: People get saved and it's totally obvious that God is doing the saving. Our faith is built because we see him answering prayer and doing things among us that could only be the mighty work of him who holds the word and the world in his right hand. It's scary encouraging. Who wants to be saved because of a church program or some humanistic evangelism training? The truth is God wants people to be saved so badly that he'll even use our false motives to bring salvation. But there's a difference when people are being saved because of answered prayers. There's a difference in a church that starts growing because God started thundering back their prayers for their town. What will the place of prayer be in your life?

This chapter is a good metaphor for what prayer does. Our prayers take the things we don't understand and put them in the context of God's word so we can see what he is doing and even join in his work. The answers God reveals almost never look like what we would expect and so answered prayers, like the book of Revelation, wake us up out of the slumber of religiosity and bring us into the grandeur of God's heavenly work on the earth. How will God answer your prayers for the lost in your life? The only way to find out is to start praying.

Week 2: In the Field Training

Peek at the Week

This week is all about prayer so you know it's going to be amazing! There are two main tasks:

1. Declare a prayer spot or prayer spots. Put them on your mission map. You can inspire others with your prayer spot on social media with #HometownMissionary #PrayerSpot
2. Make a Prayer Banner for your prayer spot. You can hang it up or keep it in your Bible or car if your prayer spot is outdoors. Or make your prayer spot mobile by taking a picture of it with your phone.

> *As you go through the training devotionals this week, you'll fill in the prayer banner.*

Make your prayer a family affair!

- Sing!
- Read Exodus 17:8-16 and have your children act it out as you read.
- Talk about prayer and answer questions your children may have about prayer.
- Make your own prayer banners and hang them up (See Tuesday's devotional time for more information).
- Go for a prayer walk and pray for the people in your family's life that you want to reach out to.
- Declare a family prayer spot.

Monday: The Place of Meeting _____

Read

Exodus 33:7-11

Examine

Moses is widely regarded as one of the greatest leaders in history. We know his skill in leadership did not come from his great speaking ability or his vision or charisma. His success was forged through conversations with God (prayer!). He led like no one else because he spoke to God like no one else.

Although God had been working in his life from his birth, Moses' first recognizable encounter with God happened on the holy ground of Mount Sinai through the burning bush. He heard God speak and he spoke back. Later, Moses would demand that God show him his glory. And God grants his request! He puts Moses in a cleft in a rock and passes by so that Moses can see the trail that the presence of God leaves behind. Even after death, Moses appears on a different mountaintop with Elijah to comfort Jesus and confuse Peter during the transfiguration.

We might long for similar mountaintop prayer experiences ourselves. But today's passage shows the day-to-day prayer work that leads to the occasional mountaintop experience. Wherever Israel camped, Moses would build his own little tent of meeting away from everyone else where he could go and talk to God. He had a conversational relationship with God—a prayer life! God was like a best friend to Moses. Such a relationship could only be forged with the priority and consistency that must have come from building a tent of meeting at every spot Israel camped.

A real prayer life is inspiring. The Israelites would watch for Moses so that when he prayed they could pray too. Can you imagine this one man going to pray and then all of Israel bowing to God at the entrances to their tents? Joshua becomes Israel's next leader and oversees the military campaign for the promised land, defeating 31 kingdoms. How does he become such an amazing leader while wandering around in a desert with a million former slaves? "Joshua the son of Nun, a young man, would not depart from the tent." He devoted himself to being in the place of prayer.

Apply

Where is your tent of meeting, your prayer spot? Do you have a place where God is waiting for you so you can converse together?

Who are the people in your life that could be inspired by your prayer life? Are your family members and friends inspired to worship God because of the priority and consistency of your prayer times?

Do

Declare a Prayer Spot—a tent of meeting. It could be a room in your house. It could be the block you live on. It could be the top of a parking garage or a lonely trail in the woods. It should be somewhere special and secluded. And it should be easily accessible so you can go there as often as possible to meet with God. Is there a place on your way to or from work? Is there a room in your home or even a closet you could decorate with things that inspire you to pray?

> Go to that prayer spot and tell God that you'd like to meet him in this place regularly.

If you want to inspire others and be inspired by others, take a picture of your prayer spot and post it on social media with the hashtags #HometownMissionary #PrayerSpot. Search those hashtags to see where people are meeting with God in hometowns all over the world.

Your Prayer Spot will be the first thing you put on the Mission Map.

Yield

"Lord, this is the place where you can expect me to come and meet with you..."

Tuesday: The Lord Is My Banner _____

Read
Exodus 17:8-16

Examine

War comes to Israel early in their desert wandering and an army is rallied by Joshua and sent out. We get no details of the battle because the real fight is taking place on a nearby hill where an old man is struggling to keep his hands raised in prayer to God. If God fights for us, then our real battle is always a battle in prayer.

All day long Moses holds up his hands. His assistants, Aaron and Hur give him a rock to sit on and help hold up his arms. By the end of the day Israel has won, not by the strength of the army but by the strength of God and Moses' commitment to prayer.

Moses builds an altar to commemorate this prayer victory and calls it "The Lord Is My Banner." Armies fight under the banners of their country and their divisions. Moses chose to fight under God's banner by relying on him. You can imagine a banner stretched out between his upheld hands that simply says, "The Lord". Moses wins the fight because he stays under the banner of the Lord through prayer. We can't enter the battle for souls under the banner of self. "The battle belongs to the Lord" so our greatest weapon is prayer surrendered to God.

Apply

We get tired all the time. When was the last time you were worn out from a prayer time?

Do you have an Aaron and a Hur in your life who will help you to keep praying?

Do

Make a prayer banner for your prayer spot. You can simply fill in the one on pages 36-37, or use that one as a template to create your own. Any piece of paper will do but a longer one (8.5x14) will be better. The rest of the week we will be filling in your prayer banner. Today's task is simply to find the paper and pick a place to put it. Some suggestions: The wall of the place where you read your Bible, your ceiling above your bed, or folded into your Bible. Spend time praying in your prayer spot with your hands raised. See how long you can hold up your arms.

Yield

"Lord I will rely on you to fight my battles..."

Wednesday: The Lord's Prayer _____

Read

Luke 11:1-4

Examine

While I see little value in *mindlessly* repeating the Lord's prayer, I think we would be remiss to ignore this prayer of which Jesus said, "When you pray, say...". There is a great benefit to *mindfully* repeating the Lord's prayer and using each line as a springboard into a deeper conversation with God. I often pray through this prayer at my prayer spot and it goes like this:

Father... then I spend time praying about how God is my father and that makes me his son, his beloved that he's always cared for and always will. [Doing this starts my prayer time with **Connection**]

Hallowed be your name... Pray about God's holiness and righteousness and how set apart he is. These first lines put God in his proper place in our hearts; in love with us but also in control of us and everything else. Now we're ready to get deeper and more vulnerable with each following line. [After connection comes **Praise**]

*Your kingdom come...*Pray for those in your life who haven't yet found God's kingdom. Pray for him to reign over all the people and circumstances in your life. This is the Hometown Missionary part of the Lord's prayer—but there's still much more. [Start the asking/supplication part of your prayer by focusing on **The Lost**]

*Give us each day our daily bread...*After praying for others we pray for ourselves and our needs. That order is important! This is where the Lord's Prayer really starts to make us vulnerable before God. Vulnerable literally means woundable. It's the opposite of being guarded or defensive. It only happens when we trust enough to put ourselves out there in a situation where we might get hurt. To tell God that he's in charge of meeting our daily needs (and therefore we aren't) is extremely vulnerable. We're taking the chance that God may let us down. But of course, he will always meet our needs! [Tell God all of your **Needs**]

*Forgive us our sins...*Even more vulnerable! After telling God how needy we are we tell him all the ways that we have sinned and the character sins we struggle with. We're letting God in on how we see ourselves even though he sees us more clearly than we ever will. It's wound-ability that puts us in touch with how much we need God. [**Confession**]

We forgive everyone... Talk about woundable; this part is often painful for me as Jesus is asking me to regularly consider the people who have hurt me so I can forgive them. It's another step deeper into vulnerability. [**Forgiveness**]

Lead us not into temptation... Last we pray through things that often tempt us to sin. We pray through our character flaws and struggles. Who do you have in your life that you can share your desires, needs, sins, hurts and flaws with? Probably very few people could handle all of that on a regular basis. So Jesus instructs his disciples to tell it all to God. This prayer is the script of an intimate relationship with the Father that isn't afraid to bear all. This is a heavenly mirror into our souls that if prayed with passion, authenticity and frequency can give us a clear picture of who we are in Christ. [End your prayer time by asking for God to **Lead**]

Apply

How vulnerable are you before God? If your prayers were God's only way of knowing you, would you be a stranger to God or a friend?

Do

Put the Lord's prayer and reminders about what each section means on your prayer banner. In your prayer spot pray through the Lord's prayer. **In the "Your Kingdom Come" section write down as many names as possible of people you want God to reign over.**

Yield

"Father, hallowed be your name..."

Thursday: The High Priestly Prayer

Read

Leviticus 16:29-34

John 17

Examine

When you read Leviticus (which you should because it is an amazing riveting book!), God's pattern for offerings is hard to miss. At the tabernacle/temple and at the festivals, the priests have to offer multiple sacrifices. First, the high priest sacrifices for himself, then for the rest of the priesthood, and then for the rest of God's people. On the Day of Atonement everything stops (including eating and working) and even those who are visitors in the land witness the high priest make these sacrifices so that first he himself, then his fellow priests and finally the rest of God's people could be atoned (literally "at oned" or made one with God again as a result of the removal of sin).

The significance of Jesus' prayer in John 17 can't be overstated, especially in light of this contextual background from Leviticus. Jesus is wrapping up the last supper and he prays this prayer that has become known as the High Priestly Prayer. If you look at the three paragraphs of this, the longest of Jesus' recorded prayers, you see that first he prays for himself, then for his disciples and then for all of God's future people. It's as if he's preparing for the sacrifice on the day of atonement except in this case, he is both the high priest and the sacrifice that makes us "at one" with God.

Just as we learned to pray through the Lord's Prayer yesterday, we can pray through the High Priestly Prayer.

We start by praising Jesus our high priest *"who always lives to intercede for us"* (Hebrews 7:25) and our sacrificial lamb. He prayed to glorify God and to be glorified by God for accomplishing the work God set before him; the saving of our souls. **Praise God for Jesus for as long as you can as you begin your prayer.**

Next Jesus prays for his disciples. These are the ones that God has given him but who will be left without his physical presence in a world that does not glorify God. They have been given God's true word and he prays for them to be sanctified (made holy) as they are sent out into the lost world that will at times hate them.

You can pray for all of your brothers and sisters in Christ who have the word and the Spirit and are being sanctified in this life as they go out into the world trying to overcome it with good instead of being overcome with evil. **Pray for your discipleship group and your church.**

Last Jesus prays for us! If you are a disciple of Jesus, then you are an answer to Jesus' High Priestly Prayer as one of *"those who will believe in me through [the disciples] word."* He wants these future followers to be united so the world can see God in their lives and so that God can continually be made known to the world by Jesus even after he is physically gone. **You can end your High Priestly Prayer by praying for the lost to know God. Pray for all the churches to become more united instead of more divided. Pray specifically for the people in your life that you could show them the love of Christ every day.**

Apply

How does it make you feel that Jesus prayed for you on the night he was betrayed?

How does this prayer relieve the pressure you feel at times about sharing your faith since the saving work of God began long before we existed?

How does this cause you to see the power and importance of praying for people, that Jesus would spend some of his last breaths on earth in prayer for himself, the disciples and the lost who would be found?

Do

Write the parts of the High Priestly Prayer on your Prayer Banner and pray through it.

Yield

"Father, the hour has come for glory…"

Friday: The Work of Prayer

Read
Nehemiah 1:1-2:4

Examine

What if we stopped praying prayers of last resort? Those are the prayers we say *after* we've done everything in our power to change a situation or a person.

You know when you finally give up and say, "Well all I can do now is pray." What if instead, we prayed prayers of first resort; we prayed before we did anything at all? What if we didn't wait until we exhausted our power to ask for power from on high but we started with God then we acted?

Nehemiah was in a position where all he could do was pray. He was 1000 miles away from his home and could only hear reports about the state of Jerusalem with no power to change anything. But he prayed, and God worked. "As soon as" he heard the report he prayed. And God made a way for him to go back and rebuild what was broken down. We often have it backwards. We don't see prayer as effective or as work. If we *only* pray about something we feel like we're being lazy. Prayer is the most powerful action we can take. Prayer is not passive. It is doing something; the best possible thing in fact.

When we commit to praying first and acting second, there is an amazing side effect that occurs. We get to see how God answers our prayer work. Nehemiah prayed and prayed. He had no idea how or if God would answer him. But one day as he was serving as cupbearer the king noticed that he was downcast. God caused the king to see and respond to the look on Nehemiah's face in order to set in motion answered prayer. I bet Nehemiah would have never guessed that God would answer his prayer in such a way. When we commit to prayer, we are trusting God that he will work on our behalf without knowing when or how. In this way our prayer lives build our faith and trust in the one we cry out to.

Apply

Is there something or someone you've been working on impacting but have been neglecting to pray for?

Can you think of any ways that God has recently answered your prayers, maybe in unexpected ways?

If you can't think of any answered prayers, you need to keep praying!

Do

Pray and do nothing. Spend time working in prayer for people and situations and then be watchful for God to work.

Write down 3 of your most important prayers on your prayer banner. Keep praying and pay attention so you can write down how God answers your prayers.

Yield

"Lord, I trust you to work on these prayers…"

Saturday: Pray For Me _____

Read
Ephesians 6:18-20

Examine
At the end of his amazing description of the armor of God, Paul launches into a plea for prayer. Paul, the super-apostle, begged for the prayers of the Ephesian church so that he could be bold in proclaiming the good news. Paul believed in prayer. He wanted the church in Ephesus to pray in the spirit, to pray for each other and to pray for him.

Are we praying for each other? When someone asks for prayer do you do it? Do you believe in the power of that prayer? Do you ask for prayer early and often when you have needs? Sure, we can pray about our own needs but there must be something about asking for prayer that pleases God and magnifies the power of prayer. Otherwise, why would Paul beg for prayers?

We saw in the Lord's prayer that the prayer Jesus taught his disciples led to greater vulnerability with God. When we ask for prayer we are being vulnerable (humble) with one another. God blesses humility. He blesses us when we ask for prayer.

Apply
Is your church a praying church? You might not be able to change your whole church but what if you just changed yourself and devoted yourself to prayer? How much would just one praying person be able to affect the entire church?

Do
The last part of your prayer banner is the "Pray For Me!" section. **Write down some things you need prayer for, *rip it out of the book* (or your own prayer banner) and bring it to church tomorrow. Trade your prayers with someone else and tape their prayer requests to that spot.**

Pray through your completed Prayer Banner

Yield
"Lord, you are my banner…"

Week 3: The Power of the Gospel

"Now after John was arrested, Jesus came into Galilee, proclaiming the gospel of God, and saying, "The time is fulfilled, and the kingdom of God is at hand; repent and believe in the gospel."

—Mark 1:14-15

Recently, my kids and I were talking about how dogs can only see in black and white. (How did scientists figure that out?!) Anyway, we all felt sad for dogs. They don't get to see the beauty of a blue sky or a sunset. The vibrancy of the leaves in fall is muted. Even rainbows look depressing in black and white!

There's something even more vibrant and beautiful and powerful than all the colors in the world and the unfortunate truth is that most people and even many Christians can't see it. What I'm talking about is the Gospel and many of us are color blind when it come to seeing the gospel. This chapter and this week's training is going to fix that!

It's essential for us to know, teach, live and breathe the gospel. How do I know gospel is this important? Because of what Paul wrote in Romans 1:16:

"For I am not ashamed of the gospel, for it is the power of God for salvation to everyone who believes, to the Jew first and also to the Greek."

So what is the gospel? Seriously. Can you answer that simple question with confidence?

What is the good news of Christ? For much of my Christian life I understood parts of the gospel and I really understood the response we should have to the gospel (Acts 2:38-41), but I did not really know the gospel which is the power of

God for salvation!

The word *gospel* means good news. It comes from the Greek *evangelion*, where we get the word evangelist. So I've been appointed a "good news-ist"! This may surprise you but historically, the good news of Jesus Christ is not the first instance of gospel in our world. An evangelion (the proclamation of the good news) was used by the Roman Empire before Jesus.

The most famous example of Roman good news was just after the death of Julius Caesar in 44 BC, so 75 years or so before Jesus died. Julius was assassinated by a political rival named Brutus (should have seen that coming with a friend named Brutus!). A civil war was sparked. Brutus' forces fought against Mark Antony and Octavius who defeated Brutus the assassin. Eventually Antony committed suicide and Octavius became Emperor (changing his name to Augustus Caesar). He began the *Pax Romana* or Roman Peace that provided relative peace and stability by the hand of a strong military for the Roman Empire for over 200 years.

All of that history may have confused you or bored you. Regardless of how far back in your head your eyes roll when you read about historical events, we can't deny the impact of Julius and Augustus Caesar and the evangelion that came after the civil war: Every summer our calendars bear their names in July and August.

The people living during that civil war and Augustus' rise to power couldn't look back and see what happened like we do now. That history-filled paragraph was written in past tense but they were experiencing these things in real time. *That's the difference* between history and news. It's history to us. It was news to them. Without twitter or television they had to rely on messengers to bring news/gospel/evangelion to their towns.

You can imagine what that must have been like: There's been a civil war and now you hear that there's a new king and that he has pledged to bring peace and prosperity to the kingdom. You hear the news and it fills you with wonder. What will this new reign be like? How will our lives be changed? Maybe everything will be different under this new king!

There's a period between hearing the news and actually seeing the changes that the news may cause. This is still true in our world today. In politics, we wonder what good or bad will come from new leadership on the news of an election. Actual change takes longer, if it happens at all. In the same way, on a personal level, when we get good news about a promotion or bad news about an illness, we face a waiting period between the announcement of the news and the actual impact.

All of that background information is to help illuminate for you the one verse on which this entire chapter is focused. My hope is that Jesus' proclamation of the good news in Mark 1:15 will become a verse that you understand more than ever before and cherish for the rest of your life.

The very first words we hear from Jesus are, *"The time is fulfilled, and the kingdom of God is at hand; repent and believe in the gospel/good news."* We know the importance of last words but have you ever considered the importance of first words? When Mark wrote his gospel he carefully chose this sentence to be the very first thing we hear Jesus say. We can't gloss over this sentence and move quickly to the calling of the first disciples. Without the proclamation of the gospel there are no disciples.

Jesus' proclamation of good news is only one sentence. Even in this he shows us the humility that would eventually allow him to submit even to death on the cross. One sentence and he borrows the pre-established method of evangelion. This isn't even inventive! But it's revolutionary! He took this well-known concept and applied it to himself (and in the process transformed it and glorified it to the utmost). He claims over and over again that his life is gospel. His very presence on the earth is the good news. Understanding the historical concept of evangelion should illuminate this claim even more.

Jesus wasn't just saying he has good news, like when your spouse tells you good news about your tax refund. Jesus was proclaiming that after centuries of war and strife and fighting against God, a new king had begun to reign; Jesus himself! And this heavenly king wouldn't just bring relative political peace for a couple of centuries but true and eternal peace to all who accepted the reign of the new king. Jesus is the good news!

The Time is Fulfilled

I want you to see the gospel in five movements. God is not far off. He is involved in our world, our history, our lives today and our futures. So we can see these five movements of the gospel in the big picture of world history, in the life of Jesus (who was the living gospel), and in our world today.

These are the 5 movements: Spirit, Creation, Fall, Redemption, Restoration. In this week's training, you'll develop the vision to see each part of the gospel in the big picture, Jesus picture, and our picture. I truly believe that this week could change your entire life if you apply yourself to see the world in gospel, the power of salvation to everyone who believes!

Everyone. Everyone in your life, is somewhere in these movements of gospel. They are experiencing gospel whether they know it or not; whether they believe it or not. If you can see gospel, you can help them see Jesus and receive salvation. This week you'll take a deep dive into each of the movements of the gospel but here's a crash course to help you understand Jesus' first words better. Gospel is:

Spirit: The Holy Spirit initiates every movement of the gospel. Before creation, in Genesis 1:2, the Spirit hovered over the waters. As we think about being Hometown Missionaries, it should take pressure off of us to know that the Spirit is who works the gospel and brings salvation—not us.

Creation: God created a good world in his image and for a little while two people lived in this perfectly good time just after the Spirit created everything. The Spirit is still creating opportunities all around us for gospel. Yet, like the first people we mar his good creation with sin when we...

Fall: This is the bad news (opposite of gospel but part of the gospel because of God's grace). We were given freedom to choose and we chose to rebel against God and his authority as creator and ruler of our lives. The first people did this and every person ever since has rebelled. We've been at war with God our creator. Immediately after the fall God reveals that he planned all along to redeem his fallen people. When you read the Old Testament, you are reading about people who lived in the time between the fall and redemption.

Redemption: This is what Jesus brought. This is the essence of the good news. You sold out to sin but you can be bought back, purchased by the blood of Christ. The civil war is over between God and humanity and God has won. Jesus came to accomplish this and the first disciples were messengers sent out (apostles) to proclaim the good news about king Jesus winning the war and gaining our redemption.

Restoration: As Jesus said in those first words in Mark, *"The time is fulfilled."* The good news is pronounced, but its full affect is still unknown. So we live in this moment between redemption and the restoration which is still to come. We've heard the news and we believe it. There is a new king in town. There is lasting peace. But we don't fully see the impact and change yet, do we? Just as our Old Testament ancestors lived in between the fall and redemption and wondered what redemption could be like, we live between redemption and the restoration of all things. We live in the period of hearing the good news but not completely understanding what it will mean for our lives and our world. We wonder what Restoration might look like and eagerly await the day when God will show it to us.

> *Right now, our world is still broken and dying and desperate because it hasn't heard or it hasn't accepted the good news. Guess what God's plan is to change that? Or I should say who is God's plan to change that? It's us! We are the messengers of the good news. We have in this news the "power of God for salvation for everyone*

who believes." When Jesus comes back that won't be true anymore. This is the era of gospel power. This is the time fulfilled.

Repent and believe the Good News

After proclaiming a new epoch of time; the era of redemption in which we now live, Jesus says, *"Repent and believe the good news."* His life, death and resurrection are an opportunity for us to change (that's what it means to repent) and to believe the good news. But since we still live in this era between redemption and restoration, the gospel is still news, it's not history...yet.

News is alive, it's in the moment, it isn't something you look back at through the lens of history. It's not something you study. It's something you react to in the moment. Jesus came proclaiming and we still proclaim that there IS good news. Not that there was good news. That would be history. The day is coming when it will all be history. But this is not that day! (2 Peter 3:8-13)

Let's get personal. What's the gospel for you? Something that happened? 2000 years ago, 5 years ago or 30 years ago when you were first saved? Either way that's not news, that's history. Or...is the gospel happening? Is the word of God living and active in your day-to-day life? That's news! That's good news!

Let's be honest. History can be boring. That paragraph about Octavius and Brutus is one of the most boring paragraphs in this whole book! I studied history in college and I was bored all the time! If the gospel is only something that happened then nobody is going to respond to it. We learn about history, appreciate it, ignore it—but it usually doesn't affect us.

News is different. News affects us. We are scandalized by it or shocked or encouraged. There's a reason that more than ever the news itself makes the news.

If you want to be a missionary in your hometown, you have to think about what you are presenting to those who need Jesus. A historic figure who taught good things or the son of God who died and didn't stay dead and is still alive today as evidenced by your life?

You know the right answer, you may even speak the right answer, but this is the trick with sharing the good news: it doesn't so much matter what you say. It matters how you live. History is conveyed with words. News is viral, spread in real life.

So what are you presenting to people who need Jesus? Words about the founder of Christianity or the example of a life lit up by the son of the living God, Jesus Christ?

Interestingly, even Jesus himself doesn't really preach the words of the gospel. He proclaims that he **IS** the gospel. It's good news, not good history. You want to be fruitful, to impact others for Christ? You don't need the words to say or even the best scriptures to use as if the Bible was a manual or textbook. You need Jesus, whom the gospel declares is still alive, to be alive in you as you go to work, school, play, home, even at church. The Holy Spirit will take over and preach the good news for you!

The Kingdom of God is at Hand

In the middle of this gospel sentence, Jesus proclaims that the *"Kingdom of God is at hand."* Then he says repent—change your outlook and life. Just as Augustus Caesar had proclaimed himself the new ruler of the Empire, Jesus claims that God's kingdom has a new king. King Jesus himself.

We've seen that Jesus ushered in a new era in time: the time of redemption before restoration. We've seen that it is still news—as long as we live fully alive for Jesus. And now we see how we can respond to that news and come to faith, repentance and life. As hometown missionaries this is the essence from Jesus himself of how we help others to respond to the gospel. Jesus answers for us in one part of one sentence what it looks like to repent and believe in the gospel:

> *We have to accept King Jesus. The kingdom of God is at hand; in your midst.*

You can imagine that some may have been disheartened by the news of Augustus and worried about his reign or even been dismissive of it, not caring. We face the same attitudes when we share the good news of Jesus Christ. People don't want lordship, or they don't care, or they want self rule. But accepting Jesus means making Jesus Lord. Saying "The kingdom of God is at hand" or in your midst is the self-proclamation of a new king.

When we share the gospel with friends and family, it may begin with an invitation to church or to some special event or maybe a meal at our home. What we're really doing is we're bringing people into the midst of the kingdom. When they come to a church event or into our homes, they are leaving the world and entering a new kingdom—a place where Jesus rules.

This is why it's so important for us to come to the meetings of the body ready to give and love and serve and look out for people who are sitting alone or looking lost or sad. Sunday morning isn't the weekly gospel sing-a-long with a cute Bible teaching. It's the kingdom of God that Jesus established with his life and blood.

Even the Chinese government understands this. They recently passed a law that churches can't display crosses. They see the cross of Christ as the flag of a foreign country, an invader with different ideals. And that's exactly what it is! Maybe they're reading the Bible more closely than us!

This is why it's so important for us to have a Christian household and not just a house that goes to church. It's bigger than our spouses and kids and roommates. We've got a new nationality and allegiance when our homes are truly devoted to King Jesus.

And this is why when we share the gospel it has to go beyond merely inviting someone to church and it needs to become Bible study and prayer and life together. (See Appendix A on page 224, for the Old School Bible study series.) We have not been commissioned to bring people to a holy club or make their lives easier or nicer. We have been commissioned to make disciples of king Jesus. We get to help bring people from self-rule, to Jesus Kingdom rule. When we study the Bible with someone we are not presenting membership requirements, we are watching God convert a soul. It's a transfer of loyalty (faith) from self to Jesus as Lord.

Did you know that as a disciple of Jesus Christ, a hometown missionary, it's your God-given, spirit enabled mission to help the people in your life choose king Jesus?

How does that make you feel? Maybe a little overwhelmed, a little intimidated, even a little hopeless? You may think "Why me?" And God did choose you out of all of your friends to reach all of your friends. How can any of us possibly help someone change allegiances and come under the lordship of Jesus Christ?

"For I am not ashamed of the gospel, for it is the power of God for salvation to everyone who believes, to the Jew first and also to the Greek."

Read that verse closely. It's not us. It's the gospel! That's why this week's training is so crucial. It's the difference between seeing the power of the gospel and relying on the power of self. If you could see the gospel, (and by the end of this week you can!) you could unleash the good news of Jesus Christ and the power of God for salvation everywhere you go.

The time is fulfilled, and the kingdom of God is at hand; repent and believe in the gospel.

Week 3: In the Field Training

Peek at the Week

The goal of this week's training is ambitious to say the least: Change the way you see everything. That's how powerful the gospel is. We'll look at the 5 movements of the gospel: Spirit, Creation, Fall, Redemption and Restoration. And we'll see each movement in the big picture of our world, in the life of Jesus, the first sermon of the church (Acts 2) and in our lives and the lives of the people around us. There's a lot of reading this week because there's a lot of good news to hear!

Keep your Prayer Banner handy and keep praying for the kingdom to come to the people in the center of your banner. Seeing the world in gospel will help you see what the Spirit may be doing in their lives so you can minister to them according to which gospel movement they are experiencing. That will make more sense by Friday!

As you go through the devotionals, you'll fill in the **Gospel Vision Chart** (at the end of this week's devotionals) that will help you see *"the power of God for salvation to everyone who believes"* (Romans 1:16). Bolded text should provide you with the hints you need to complete this task. **On the last day, you'll write out your testimony through the lens of these Gospel movements.**

#ISeeGospel

This week's social media challenge is going to be fun! As you learn to see Spirit, Creation, Fall, Redemption and Restoration take a picture of these movements and post it with the hashtags #HometownMissionary #ISeeGospel. You'll get it as you read the devotionals and you'll see examples from your brothers and sisters by searching these hashtags. Sharing your testimony with this hashtag at the end of the week should be the first time you share your faith since starting this training. You'll be amazed at what the gospel can do when we know it and share it.

Teach your family the Good News of Jesus!

- Sing!
- Talk about the movements of the gospel with your family in an age appropriate way.
- Take a walk and look for the movements of Gospel on your walk. Take pictures.
  - Spirit—look for ways that invisible things have an effect like wind or sunlight

- ○ Creation—is there something new being built or is something growing or blooming?
- ○ Fall—is something dying, closed or falling?
- ○ Redemption—do you see anything that makes you think about Jesus?
- ○ Restoration—is there something that was closed or dead that has new life?
- • When you get home, take a look at the pictures you took and talk about the gospel.
- • Pray together

Fill out the **Gospel Vision Chart** at the end of this chapter to see the gospel more clearly.

Monday: Spirit

Read
Genesis 1:1-2
Mark 1:9-13
Acts 2:1-4, 16-21
Acts 11:15-18

Examine
It all starts with the Spirit, literally. Through the Holy Spirit, God interacts with his creation. Without the Spirit's initiative we would never realize our lostness (John 16:8-11), seek after God (Romans 3:11), or repent (Acts 11:18). Any hope we have in this world is because of the Holy Spirit's work. Spirit is a word we do not hear enough or speak enough. This may partly be due to the very nature of the Spirit himself. His role in the trinity is to illuminate the Father and the Son. He's content to stay in the background and promote God and Jesus. But we should not allow the Spirit to stay behind the scenes in our lives. The Spirit is the starting point of the gospel.

It should not surprise us then, that in the **big picture, meta-narrative** of the Bible, the Spirit shows up in the second verse of scripture. When the world is formless and empty and chaotic, the Spirit of God is there and is intimately involved with God's creating work. The Spirit was present and active in our world long before the indwelling we experience today. He was involved in the Exodus, the tabernacle and temple, the transfer of the kingdom from Saul to David, and in the ministry of the prophets. The Spirit worked upon people who didn't even believe in God like Pharaoh and Nebuchadnezzar so that God's will would be done on the earth.

Jesus understood the necessity of the Spirit. Before he began his ministry, in which he would proclaim the gospel, live the gospel, and die the gospel, the Spirit descends upon him at his baptism and immediately drives him out into the wilderness. At the start, there's the Spirit! He's not only active, but He's urgent in His action. The word "immediately" is twice associated with what the Spirit is doing.

The Spirit powerfully initiates in **Acts 2** as well. Jesus promised that the coming of the Spirit and the kingdom would be worth the wait (Acts 1:4-8) and 10 days after his ascension to heaven the time is right for the gospel to be proclaimed to all the earth through the apostles and Peter, who had been given the keys to unlock the kingdom. But it's not Peter who initiates the kingdom, it's the Spirit. The Spirit comes down like tongues of fire and Peter gets up to preach the good news of Jesus Christ. The Holy Spirit then translates his message so that the audience from all over the world could hear the message in their own native tongue. That's how important the gospel is and that's how powerful the Spirit is. God made Google Translate available 2000 years early! Everyone needed to hear the Gospel and the Spirit was there at the start to make it possible.

The Spirit makes gospel possible. But not just in the Bible! The Spirit is active **today**. He dwells inside of believers. He still works on even the most stubborn unbelieving hearts from the outside in. The Spirit creates out of chaos. The Spirit causes urgent and immediate action. The Spirit initiates the gospel and makes it available to all people.

Apply

How do you see the Spirit working in your life? Can you see this first movement of the gospel in your world? Think about the people on your prayer banner—can you see the Spirit moving them?

Do

Take the pressure off of evangelism (good news-ism). We shouldn't really feel any pressure as we go about the mission. The Spirit is doing all the work before we ever say a word and in every word we say!

- Fill in the Spirit row of the Gospel Vision with thoughts or verses.
- Post thoughts or pictures of the Spirit working in your world with the hashtags #HometownMissionary #ISeeGospel

Yield

Lord, show me the ways that the Spirit has worked in my life as I meditate in prayer...

Show me what the Spirit may be doing in the lives of my friends...

Tuesday: Creation

Read
Genesis 1:1-2
Matthew 1:1, 1:18
Acts 2:22

The Spirit was present at creation and never left. Creation is the next movement of the gospel. We are quite familiar with the **big picture biblical** creation account in Genesis 1. God made our good world that culminated in the creation of mankind in his own image. His creation was perfect and without blemish because he is perfect and without blemish. Mankind was created with purpose and choice. Purpose: to be fruitful and multiply and rule (care for) creation. Choice: to obey God or rebel and find our own way. More on that in the next movement!

It all begins in Genesis, which gets its name from the Greek word for beginnings. It all begins again in Matthew. In Greek, the word "genealogy" in Matthew 1:1 is the word genesis. So Matthew 1:1 could be read: "The book of Genesis of Jesus Christ". Think about that for a moment. What a bold way to start the New Testament! Jesus is a new beginning; the genesis of a new opportunity from the Spirit for all of mankind to be saved.

Jesus' conception and birth by the power of the Holy Spirit is the spark of this 2nd movement of the gospel. In a sense, the incarnation of **Jesus** is not a new creation, but the pinnacle of creation. Jesus' life shows us what it means to live as an image bearer of God and what we could be without sin. Like God and the Spirit, Jesus is eternal and therefore uncreated, but he has inserted himself into our world, *"being born in the likeness of men"* (Philippians 4:7). In this, he has created for us an opportunity to become what we were created to be.

In **Acts 2:22,** Peter begins his Spirit inspired gospel message by talking about Jesus. Think about all that God has created from the life of Jesus Christ! He is still doing mighty works and wonders and signs to this day though the life of one man who walked the earth almost 2000 years ago!

Creation is not merely an idea written on the pages of the Bible. Creation is happening **all around us.** My regular prayer walks in the woods cause me to marvel at God's creation again and again. A gospel fluent person can see creation in their own lives and in the lives of the people they interact with. A family moves in next door: When we are immersed in gospel, we see God creating a new relationship. A loved one gets ill: Gospel teaches us that God is creating an opportunity to show the love of Christ to the sick person (Mark 1:30-31). You lose your job: It might feel like a setback but it's also God creating an opportunity to show his glory through you in a new workplace. God's act of creation is so powerful that it's still happening all around us.

Apply

Where do you see creation happening in your life? Can you see this 2nd movement of the gospel in your world? Think about the people on your prayer banner. Can you see what God may be creating in their lives to help them respond to the gospel?

Do

Take a walk in God's creation and thank him for all the new beginnings in your life.

- Fill in the **Creation** section of the Gospel Vision with thoughts or verses.
- Post your thoughts or any pictures of **Creation** with the hashtags #HometownMissionary #ISeeGospel

Yield

Father I praise you for your creation, that I am one of your beloved creatures, that my friends and family we created lovingly by and for you...

Wednesday: Fall _____

Read

Genesis 2:15-17, 3:1-8
Romans 3:23, 6:23, 8:19-22
Acts 2:23

The fall caused by our sin is the bad news part of the good news. Unfortunately, it's just as undeniable as creation itself.

We know what mankind does when given a choice. We read about Adam and

Eve in scripture but we also know plenty about the fall because we ourselves so often choose rebellion and sin instead of following God's good way. All of creation (**really big picture!**) is tied together with humanity's fall. Our rebellion doesn't just affect us. All of God's good world is subjected to the consequences of sin (depleted glory, separation from God, and death). Where I live in Michigan, this cycle of death in creation is put on vivid display every fall as the leaves gloriously change color and then fall to the ground dead.

Our Fall immediately follows creation in Genesis and is proclaimed in **Peter's Pentecost sermon,** *"This Jesus, delivered up according to the definite plan and foreknowledge of God, you crucified and killed by the hands of lawless men"* (Acts 2:23). When confronted with God's perfection, humanity acts predictably: we rebel, sending Jesus to the cross. But all of this falls within the gospel. It's all part of God's plan. Jesus was born as God's preordained response to our rejection of him and his way. So even the bad news is good news by the power of gospel! Even the terrible day on which our fallen nature and sin killed the Son of God is called Good Friday because of the power of the gospel!

Just as we can look through gospel eyes and see creation happening all around us, we can also see the fall in everything. **We sin. We rebel.** We see the mighty works of God and we chose our own way, anyway. We see this in ourselves and we are affected by it in others. We even see it in the headlines on a daily basis. God's creation is tainted by sin. The world is not filled with the image bearers God created his people to be. It is certainly not perfect. It isn't even "very good." But this is what puts the good in the good news. If this were the final movement of the gospel, we should be quite depressed. But there's more to the gospel. The killing of Jesus that Peter charges the crowd with is the worst act of sin and rebellion of all and all of humanity is guilty. Yet, when we were at our worst, he made it the best. You'll see tomorrow!

Apply

Where do you see **The Fall or Sin** and its effects in your life? Can you see this 3rd movement of the gospel in this broken world? Think about the people on your prayer banner—can you see how they might be breaking God's heart by rebelling and choosing their own way? In the power of his mercy do you see how these people's sin could eventually lead them to seek after God?

Do

Pray specifically through your sin and the sins you see in the people on your prayer list. Don't judge yourself or them—just thank God for Jesus, who died for

each of those sins and each of those people.
- Fill in the **Fall** section of the Gospel Vision Sheet with thoughts or verses.
- Post thoughts or pictures of **Fall** with the hashtags #HometownMissionary #ISeeGospel

Yield

Lord, here are the ways I fall and fall again, but no matter what, help me to always fall on my knees before you...

Use even the sin in the lives of my friends to bring them to you...

Thursday: Redemption

Read
Genesis 3:15
John 14:6
Hebrews 11:39-40
Acts 2:24
1 Peter 2:4-10

Examine

Even in his condemnation of Adam, Eve and the Serpent, God provides a glimpse of his great plan of redemption. He tells the Serpent that there are now two seeds of people on the earth: The serpent's offspring tied hopelessly to the creation/death cycle and Eve's offspring through which God would work a mighty plan of redemption but not without suffering himself (Genesis 3:15). The Bible's big picture is the story of how God worked to redeem his people through Abraham and Moses and David and many more humble heroes and struggling saints. Throughout the majority of scripture, God's people did not know how they would be redeemed from the fall and its deserved consequences. How blessed are we to now know that redemption is only possible through faith in **Jesus** Christ! (John 14:6).

The moment that mankind could finally understand God's plan of redemption is on Pentecost during Peter's Holy Spirit translated, first day of the church, keys to the kingdom sermon, that we've been working through. After **Peter** tells the people what we did to Jesus by giving him the death sentence we deserved, he explains that God was using that same moment of hatred and injustice to save our souls in the most powerful way. *"God raised him up, loosing the pangs of death, because it was not possible for him to be held by it"* (Acts 2:24). Jesus overcame death! Peter goes on to quote the Psalms and ends his message by proving the resurrection from the scriptures. Resurrection may seem normal to us because we hear about it in church all the time (we are inoculated against it making it benign/ineffectual) but for Peter's audience, resurrection was the faith hurdle they needed to overcome. It was an unbelievable and scandalous idea that was either the biggest lie ever told or a fact that would change the whole world.

Redemption has to do with being bought back (redeemed). Our sin earns us death but the death of Christ as the perfect lamb of God buys us back from death and gives us life. How do we know? Resurrection! Those who believed made Jesus their Lord by repenting (changing their way to Jesus' way) and being baptized. They were added to the church and received the Holy Spirit (Of course! The Spirit is always involved in new creation!).

If we believe the gospel, we can see Spirit, creation and fall **all around us**. But unlike the first three movements of the gospel, we only see redemption if we share the gospel with the lost. A group of people immersed in the gospel (a true church) will see many people redeemed by the blood of Jesus through faith, repentance and immersion in the waters of baptism. But if we can't see gospel all around us we end up living in the creation/death cycle that Jesus came to free us from. Redemption, what the ancients longed for, is all about resurrection and new life. But so far in the Bible and in our world there's only been one eternal resurrection. That means there must be one more movement of Gospel to truly make this Good News.

Apply

Where do you see **Redemption** in your life? How has the redemptive work of Christ on the cross and in the resurrection changed you? Think about the people on your prayer banner—can you envision what their lives would look like redeemed by God?

Do

Praise God in prayer for all the ways he's redeemed you. Beg God to redeem those around you from all the sin that is keeping them from coming close to God and being saved.

- Fill in the **Redemption** section of the Gospel Vision with thoughts or verses.
- Post your thoughts or any pictures of **Redemption** with the hashtags #HometownMissionary #ISeeGospel

Yield

Lord, Jesus' death and resurrection has bought me back from sin and I praise you...

These people in my life desperately need your redemption...

Friday: Restoration

Read
Genesis 2:8-10
Revelation 21:1-5, 22:1-5
Romans 8:22-30

God's not done yet. The **big picture** view of the Bible starts and ends in a garden where people live in the presence of God unhindered by sin. We aren't there yet but that's where all of this is going. God is going to restore his creation. He's going to make it like new. Paul talks about how redeemed Christians still have God's restoration to look forward to, saying, *"For we know that the whole creation has been groaning together in the pains of childbirth until now. And not only the creation, but we ourselves, who have the first fruits of the Spirit, groan inwardly as we wait eagerly for adoption as sons, the redemption of our bodies"* (Romans 8:22-30).

We've already been through **Peter's** entire Pentecost sermon and the crowd's salvation response. So where does Acts 2 mention this fully restorative-redemption to come? Jesus died on the weekend of the Passover festival in the spring. How fitting and ironic (divine!) that Jesus, the firstborn son of God, would die as a sacrificial lamb for our sins as the people of God were celebrating the "passing over" of Israel's firstborn sons by eating sacrificed lambs. That final plague of death on Egypt led to their redemption from slavery. Of course, this Passover/crucifixion connection is well known. The connection between Jesus and the next major Jewish Holy Day is less known but just as significant.

Pentecost (from the Greek word 50th) is that next Holy Day. It's 50 days after passover and it's also known as "First Fruits." It was a celebration of the very first grain that could be harvested and a faithful anticipation that the rest of the harvest would soon follow. **Jesus** was the Passover lamb and he is also the first fruit. The festival itself and the timing of the Holy Spirit to have Peter start the kingdom on this Pentecost holy day tells us that there is a greater harvest to come. Jesus is the firstborn/first fruit from among the dead and someday all of God's faithful offspring will also arise. Death could not keep its hold on Jesus and it won't work on us either.

We will be restored along with all of creation. We're living in between the 4th and 5th movements of the gospel and waiting for God's tomorrow; the next Holy Day when he will come back to set everything right again (more on this later in the book!).

This is perhaps the most amazing thing about seeing **our world** in gospel: Even though we await the full restoration of God, as Paul said, we have the first fruits of the Spirit now. So, just as we see glimpses of death and wrath all around us from the fall, with gospel eyes we can also see glimpses of the restoration to come. Restored marriages, restored relationships between parents and children, people restored from addiction. It's as if restoration is breaking out all the time among God's kingdom people, if you can see it. It's as if God can't help but give us previews of the glory that's coming next.

Apply

Can you see glimpses of **Restoration** in your life right now? Can you see it even amidst the brokenness caused by sin? Think about the people on your prayer banner. How glorious will restoration be when it breaks out in their lives?

Do

Praise God in prayer for all the ways God is already making things new. Dream about the day that God will return and make everything good and very good again.

- Fill in the **Restoration** section of the Gospel Vision with thoughts or verses.
- Post your thoughts or any pictures of **Restoration** with the hashtags #HometownMissionary #ISeeGospel

Yield

God, I long to see the day when you make everything new. When I dream about it I see...

Saturday: Can You See the Gospel _____

Read
Ephesians 1:11-23

Examine
This passage may contain the longest run-on sentence in the Bible but how

else do you describe something so glorious? Paul is talking about the Gospel and all of its parts so there's nothing he can do but go on and on about God's plan, the Holy Spirit, what Jesus did and how gloriously blessed we are!

Paul prayed for the church in Ephesus to have *"the eyes of your hearts enlightened, that you may know the hope to which he has called you…"* (Ephesians 1:18). This strange image, a heart with eyes, is my hope for you this week and for the rest of your life. Oh, that our hearts could see in **gospel!** That we could see the ways the **Spirit** is working in every single situation; going before us readying hearts to receive the message of Christ. That we could see **creation** happening all around us; all of these opportunities for glory springing up in the most unlikely places with just one word from God or one breath from the Spirit. That we would be more sensitive to **the fall** and the death that surrounds us, more mournful; suffering alongside those entangled in sin without judgment so God has space to unleash the power of the gospel. That we would lament the death all around and our hearts wouldn't be able to keep the gospel inside because we know what it means to be redeemed. That we'd be messengers of **redemption**; showing the wage earners of death that Jesus has offered a gift of life. That all this death would start to get bought back one soul at a time. That the broken cities we live in would start to look more and more like the garden of God. That we'd gather and long for **restoration**; our conversations transformed from bemoaning the things of this world to dreaming about the things in the next. That we'd praise and worship God every time we got a glimpse of the restoration to come in our relationships and marriages and churches. Oh how our praises would change if we could just see the restorative work of Christ more clearly, **if we could see in Gospel with the eyes of our hearts!**

Apply

At times we're asked how we got saved or what our testimony is. We might talk about who reached out to us or what we needed to change. We SHOULD talk about Gospel. How does your salvation story sound when seen through gospel eyes?

Do

Write your testimony using the 5 movements of the gospel that you learned about this week. Look over your completed Gospel Vision for ideas and inspiration. You can post your gospel testimony on social media as a creative way to share your faith and inspire future missionaries using #HometownMissionary #ISeeGospel

Yield

Lord, help me to see the world in Gospel…Show me how each movement of the gospel is being worked in my life and in the lives of the people around me…

GOSPEL VISION

	Creation	Fall	Redemption	Restoration	Spirit
Big Picture					
Jesus					
Peter's Sermon					
Your Life					
People You're Praying For					

Week 4: The Presence of Jesus

"Now the eleven disciples went to Galilee, to the mountain which Jesus had directed them. And when they saw him they worshiped him, but some doubted. And Jesus came and said to them, 'All authority in heaven and on earth has been given to me. Go therefore and make disciples of all nations, baptizing them in the name of the Father, and of the Son and of the Holy Spirit, teaching them to observe all that I have commanded you. And behold, I am with you always, to the end of the age.'"

—Matthew 28:16-20

We know these words well. You may have even skipped reading the quote above because your eyes were rolling as you saw it. "Go and make disciples of all nations." We've heard this before! You had to see this coming in a book called, "How to be a missionary in your hometown." But we're going to take a different approach to this familiar passage so unroll those eyes!

Some people are sent by God. They GO to another country and culture to make disciples. You are not one of those people right now. Unless you are reading this as a foreign missionary (may God bless your work!) then you are not going and making disciples of all nations. But this is the great commission! Do you need to pack your bags and set off on the mission? Not unless you're called! Instead we need to learn how to follow this commission right where we are and *make disciples every day and everywhere we go.*

It's one thing to know a command and a whole other thing to know how to righteously follow it. There are many times in my life as a disciple and church leader that I have followed this command but failed to follow Jesus. I'm still learning to obey everything he has taught me and I want to breathe new life into the great commission.

Some Doubted

Have you ever imagined what it would be like to spend a day with Jesus? Sometimes when I'm feeling down, I just think about how incredible that would be. Listening to him teach, watching him do miracles, all you can eat loaves and fishes. So cool.

Please put this book down for a moment and read **Mark 4:35-5:43**.

Matthew, Mark and Luke all record this day in the life of Jesus. It's as if Jesus just gets more and more amazing verse by verse. First, there's a storm on the Sea of Galilee. Jesus is sleeping through it while his disciples all think they are going to die. They wake Jesus up and he rebukes the wind. He tells the sea to be still. And the wind and the waves obey him! How would you react? I've been terrified by wind and waves on an ill advised pontoon trip with some friends into Lake Superior. It was scary. But if someone on our boat stood up and told the waves to stop and the waves listened, well that would be a whole new level of scary. I'd probably jump off the boat. The disciples are not amazed by this, they are filled with fear. And that's the right response. Would you want to be on a little boat with someone who had that kind of power?

They get off the boat and when they land on the other side of the sea, they are approached by *the most* demon possessed man. He's really more of a monster than a man, living in the hill country, crying out at night and cutting himself. He runs toward the boat yelling at Jesus. So if this were a movie, they've gone from a natural disaster thriller to a zombie horror flick. His disciples thought they were terrified on the boat with Jesus but now on the shore they have reached new levels of fear. Jesus speaks to the demon as he had to the sea. The evil spirit is stubborn so Jesus turns conversational. Jesus is having a conversation with demons! He asks the demon's name and it is revealed that there are hundreds of demons in the poor man. They work out a deal for the demons to go into a nearby herd of pigs who immediately run into the sea and drown. The townspeople come out and see the aftermath: drowned pigs and a perfectly restored wild man. They do not rejoice. They do not celebrate. They beg Jesus to get back on the boat and leave. They are afraid.

So the disciples and Jesus cross the sea again and are greeted by a clamoring crowd on the shore. Jairus, the leader of the local synagogue, has a daughter near death. Jesus and the crowd rush to heal her. But on the way he is touched by a woman who suffered with bleeding for 12 years. When she touches him, her bleeding stops and she is healed. Jesus stops to find out who touched him. The healed woman falls before him in "fear and trembling." I'm sure she was filled with joy at her healing but then to come face to face with one who can heal a decades old disease by being touched—the power of such a man is overwhelming!

This pause to identify the faithful woman was long enough for Jairus' daughter to die. But determined, Jesus presses on with the crowd to get to the girl. When he arrives at the dead girl's house there are already people mourning, Jesus tells them that the girl is only sleeping, and they actually laugh at him. He kicks them out of the house! Then he takes the dead girl by the hand, a dead body, and simply asks her to "arise". And the dead girl gets up! The crowd is overcome with amazement. He has to remind them to feed her, fearing they were too shocked to care for the revived child. And people say the Bible is boring!

Back in Matthew 28, Jesus speaks to the doubting worshipers, saying, *"All authority on heaven and on earth has been given to me."* This wasn't news. It was a reminder of what they had already seen day after day as they followed Jesus.

Jesus has authority over all of nature. He calms the storm with a word.

Jesus has authority over the dark forces of evil. He negotiates with demons and they do as he wishes.

Jesus has authority over sickness. If disease even touches him it is remedied.

He has authority even over death. He takes death by the hand and raises it to life.

Now I want you to imagine spending a day with the Jesus of the Bible—not the Cadbury egg easter Jesus from Walgreens—but the one who has all authority. It would be the most thrilling, terrifying and amazing day of your life! At times it would be down right scary. He's just so powerful.

Something that has always amazed me is that after spending years with Jesus and seeing all of his authority, and then even seeing him risen from the dead, the disciples worship but some are still doubting.

Isn't it amazing that such a verse is in the Bible? God's word is so honest! There's no way I'm putting this in my gospel if I'm Matthew. My gospel says, "Everyone believed and you should too!" But Matthew is honest. After being with Jesus and seeing him die and then not be dead anymore, the disciples still doubted, even as they worshipped.

Worshipping doubters. That's not a title limited to the eleven, is it? We worship through our doubts all the time. Maybe that's how you'd describe the way you've been worshipping God if you had the courage to be as honest as the Bible. I know that whenever I share my faith, I'm sharing through my doubts. Let's be real about our doubts because there's something Jesus needs to say to us as worshipping doubters.

All Authority

There's more than one reason why we doubt. A lack of faith is not always based on cowardice. Sometimes we don't believe because we don't want to believe. The truth and its consequences are too scary for us. It's easier to doubt than it is to truly believe. I think that's where the doubting disciples were. If they stopped doubting and truly believed that the one they were worshipping, their teacher and their friend Jesus, was actually God raised from the dead, with all the authority of God, then that would change everything. Is there anything more terrifying than change? They'd be compelled to do whatever Jesus commanded them to do. He would be their Lord. They'd "go and make disciples of all nations." But if they could convince themselves to doubt all that Jesus had done, then they could dismiss the command and the commission. They could put the Jesus chapter of their lives behind them and move on.

All Authority. We hate authority. Our nature is to rebel. We have a state police sergeant in our church who once taught us a lesson in his full uniform. Good Christian people in the audience later said that they were nervous in the presence of a uniformed officer even though he was their friend and brother. There's something about powerful authority that puts us off.

Before we accept the commission to go and make disciples everywhere we go, we have to accept the proclamation that comes before it. *"All authority in heaven and on earth has been given to me."* Do you believe that? Intellectually we do. I'm sure you believe that Jesus calmed the storm, healed the sick and raised the dead. But it's the consequence of authority, the strings attached to it that sometimes scare us and cause us to doubt. Because here's reality: if you believe that the Lord Jesus has all the authority then you must obey his command because he has all authority over you too.

> *The wind and the waves obeyed his command. 2000 demons obeyed his command. Sickness and death obeyed his command.*

Will you?

Doubt enters and tries to keep up from going and making disciples. But doubt is answered by authority. Listen!

"But you don't understand my environment! If I brought people into this church, they wouldn't be helped."

"My friends aren't open. You don't understand the **nature** of my situation!"
But Jesus has authority over all nature.

"But this guy is so far from God. He hates Jesus and church."

"My family is so lost that they persecute me. When I try to talk about God it hurts. It's like they're **demon possessed**."
But Jesus has authority over actual demons.

"But I've been **wounded**. I tried to share my faith and I '**bled**' for it."

"I was hurt by the people I shared with. I was hurt by the church."

"I'm walking wounded, scarred and scared."
Jesus has authority over our sickness and our wounds, even our wounded hearts.

"Well, if she got saved it would be like **raising the dead**."

"If he got baptized, it would be the biggest miracle the world has ever seen."
Jesus even has authority over death. And He's the biggest miracle the world has ever seen.

Here's the thing: If Jesus has all the power and authority, then how much do we have? We don't really have any. But if we have no power, how can we go and make anything?

Here's how the greatest evangelist who ever lived, the apostle Paul, shared his faith: "And I, when I came to you, brothers, did not come proclaiming to you the testimony of God with lofty speech or wisdom. **For I decided to know nothing among you except Christ Jesus and him crucified.** And I was with you in weakness and in fear and much trembling, and my speech and my message were not in plausible words of wisdom, but in demonstration of the Spirit and of power, so that your faith might not rest in the wisdom of men but in the power of God (1 Corinthians 2:1-6). When we truly accept Jesus' authority and power it leaves us in "weakness and in fear and much trembling" just like it did for his disciples and for Paul.

> *When we skip the authority part of the great commission and go straight to going and making disciples, we talk about the wrong things like technique and strategy and what we can do to be better at going and making disciples. But it's not about what we can do!*

It's about what he can do. We can't really do anything. He can do anything and everything. No wonder he counseled his disciples, *"do not be anxious about how you should defend yourself or what you should say, for the Holy Spirit will teach you in that very hour what you ought to say."* I know it's scary. Scary powerful. But it's exactly what you'd expect from a man claiming to be God. He'd have all the power. And praise God he does!

> **No person, no church, no movement has any power at all.**

It's all God and that should stir up a healthy fear in our hearts. We obey by going and making disciples of all nations, "baptizing them in the name of the Father and of the Son and of the Holy Spirit." There it is again, another reminder of who has the power. Yet we so often glance over this part too. We baptize in the name of the *Father, Son and Holy Spirit.* Have you ever really stopped to think about that part of the commission? That's more than just a formulaic saying for baptisms. What are we doing as we obey the commission of Christ? We're unleashing the power of the Holy Trinity! It's his name and his power that saves. This is a clear commentary on how we are to go about the making of disciples. It must be done by his strength and his authority. **It must actually be done in His name. To go and make disciples on our own is to disobey the command of Christ.** So how can we make disciples and baptize them by his authority and power? If it's that important, you'd think he would tell us that!

I Am With You Always

Last words matter. In the last chapter we saw the importance of first words in Mark. Matthew ends his gospel with this commission and that makes these words essential. But even the commission itself has last words and to make them even more important they contain a promise. *"And behold, I am with you always, to the end of the age."*

I love Easter. I love Easter because I love food and you get to eat so much good food. There's no distraction from opening presents like on Christmas. It's all about the meal. Christmas has become commercialized and hijacked. Somehow the free market hasn't yet figured out how to hijack Easter. Attempts to cash in on the resurrection fall short with eggs and bunnies and that fake grass that lines easter baskets. Of course, I love Easter for another reason besides the meal. I love the difference Easter makes. What we celebrate on Easter is the most amazing thing this world has ever seen. Resurrection! Is there anything more important or amazing? And Easter has a direct influence on our mission. If Jesus had not raised, we'd all be trying to be disciples and make disciples by our own power. Do you remember how much power you have? (I think we decided it was none!) So how's that mission going to work?

But Easter tells us that Jesus isn't someone who lived and had the power of God. Jesus is someone who lives and lives inside of us with all the power of God! (And this week's training devotionals will tell you the same thing!).

When I first thought about this chapter I was going to call it, "The Example of Jesus" and look at all the ways he shared his faith. And if you read the gospels, the way Jesus shared is amazing—we'll get into it in the weeks to come.

> *But more important than seeing how Jesus shared his faith when he lived on the earth, is seeing how Jesus still shares his faith now that he lives in me and you.*

If we can't do this on our own, and we need to do it with his power, then the only way we can go and make disciples is if he goes with us—**and that's exactly what the very last words of Jesus in Matthew promise.** That's what we should be celebrating each year when Easter comes around.

Imagine a kid on the playground getting bullied and he tells the bullies that his brother is really strong and he could beat them up. Maybe the bullies believe him and leave him alone. But what a difference if that child says his brother is really strong and he's standing right beside them, towering over them with a big presence.

That's the difference between talking about Jesus and taking your brother Jesus with you. You can tell people about the power of your God and some may listen, or you can show them the power of your God unleashed in your life and they will be blown away! It's not what you say or how you say it that counts so much (and for some reason that's the stuff we worry about). It's who you're with that really matters, and Jesus says, "Surely I am with you always."

Holy Days

Speaking of Christmas and Easter, I recently heard a term for Christmas and Easter Christians who only go to church on those two holidays: Keisters! There's a big difference between going to church two times a year and having Jesus with you always. But the truth is you can go to church every Sunday and still not have Jesus with you.

During Christmastime we decorate our houses and the radio stations play Christmas music and even the stores get decorated for the season. I think the most depressing hour of every year is midnight on Christmas. Often, we're driving home from family Christmas celebrations at that time and the radio station switches back from Christmas music to light rock. The transition from O Holy Night to John Cougar Mellencamp is jarring. Christmas is over just like that.

Yes, we can go to church things multiple times every week and still be Keisters in our hearts. We come in and we sing and we hug and fellowship and take communion—maybe even shout an amen or two—but then what happens next? Do we leave the presence and power of Jesus at the church so we can come visit him again on Wednesday or Sunday-or-is-he-with-you-always?!?!

You can leave a dead God wherever you want, you can visit him at his tomb, you can go to his church, but a living God, a resurrected Easter savior, well you gotta take the Lord with you everywhere you go.

And then everywhere you go it's not your power (you have none) but he can calm your storms, he can cast out those demons, he can heal and he can even raise the dead. You can go and make disciples with all of that Trinitarian authority if Jesus is with you. That's what resurrection—believing and not doubting resurrection—does. Believing that God can raise the dead and believing that Jesus is alive in you will change the world even if you never get called to leave your hometown.

To help us remember this, Jesus gave us another command. He told us to eat bread and drink the fruit of the vine, representing his body and blood. Think about that. He told us to put his body and blood inside of us, and after he conquered death he promised to be with us, to be alive inside of us, always. What a perfect reminder of his presence! Easter, Christmas, Communion every week and the Great Commission. Everything we celebrate in Jesus has something to do with Jesus in us!

This week's training devotionals are all about knowing what you can do if Jesus is alive within you everywhere you go. It's about being conscious that the risen Christ is spending every day with you. He makes us so powerful.

Peek at the Week:

This week we're starting to turn conviction into action. Even your family devotional is all about taking action to bring people into your home and show them God's love. We're also going to take our prayers and turn them into shares day by day as the presence of Jesus goes with us into our hometown missions. Inspire other hometown missionaries with **#HometownMissionary** and **#MyDayWithJesus** with a picture or story that tells the world how the presence of Jesus transformed you and helped you share.

Household Hospitality Night
Family Planner

For our family devotional this week, we'll dream and brainstorm about how we can reach out to people in our lives through hospitality. In two weeks the challenge will be to host a hospitality night! Obviously this takes a few weeks to organize effectively and to get the word out. So, before you get into this week's training devotionals, read <u>Hebrews 13:2</u> and fill out this page this week to get started and be ready!

- I will host a hospitality night on _____

OR

- I will attend a hospitality night at _____ on _____
  - If people in your church are also reading this book, you can join them instead of hosting.

- Our Hospitality Night Theme will be _____
  - Ideas:
    - Game Night
    - Sports
    - Something involving FOOD
    - Some other creative idea!

- We will invite (Write the names in the boxes below)

- We will make invitations or invite people in this way _____
  - This is a great way to get the kids involved!

After your hospitality night, add a Mission Moment to your Mission Map!

**Hospitality will be our theme in a couple of weeks so you will learn more. But for now you should know that it's not about overtly preaching the gospel but instead showing the love of Christ through your hospitality. Be creative about who you'll invite, make it special in your own way and watch how God opens doors for you to share the gospel before, during and after the event!

Prayer List → Share List

This week's devotionals will have you taking people from your prayer banner/ prayer list and putting them on this Share List. This is a way to pray more specifically about how you can share with the people that the Spirit has put on your heart. You'll be empowered by this week's reading as you see that you are never sharing alone. The living Jesus makes us able to share our faith and the gospel with everyone we're praying for! Fill this out each day when prompted.

Jesus Makes Me Strong—Tuesday

- I will share with _____ because Jesus makes me strong.

Jesus Makes Me Wise—Wednesday

- I will share with _____ because Jesus will give me wisdom. I'll start learning about _____ so I can share more effectively.

Jesus Makes Me Creative—Thursday

- I will share with _____ because Jesus makes me creative. This is how the Holy Spirit is creatively leading me to share with this person

_____.

Jesus Makes Me Honest—Friday

- I will lovingly and honestly share with _____. Even though it may be painful, Jesus will make me honest so I can tell this person that they need to hear _____ about God who loves them.

Jesus Makes Me Urgent—Saturday

- I will share as soon as possible and with gospel urgency with _____ because Jesus makes me urgent.

Week 4: In the Field Training

"Come and you will see." —Jesus (see John 1:35-51)

Jesus shared his faith with some of the early disciples that he called by simply spending a day with them. By the end of the day they were convinced that he was the Son of God and they were already sharing about Jesus with others! Almost 2000 years later, it's more than just a daydream that we might spend the day with Jesus. He promises to be "with us always". That's each and every day! This week we'll see how Jesus can make us more like him if we remember that we're not doing this alone. He is with us just as he was with the early disciples as they spread the original gospel message.

Monday: But Who Do You Say That I AM? _____

Read
Matthew 16:13-20

Examine
What a day to be with Jesus! It seems as if it is just a travel note, but there may be a great deal of significance to the place where Jesus chooses to ask his disciples these questions. The region of Caesarea Philippi is north of Galilee where at the base of a large rocky hill there is a cave where the Jordan river begins its run starting as an underground stream that emerges from the mouth of the cave. The Greeks and Romans believed this cave to be the door to Hades/Hell with the underground river being the River Styx which carried souls to the afterlife. Because of this belief, temples and idols were built into the side of the hill, the remains of which can still be visited today.

Knowing this, we can imagine this conversation happening in the midst of all of these idols. Statues of Caesar/Zeus, Hermes and Nike, with worshippers of these dead gods all around. Jesus stops his small band of disciples at this place and asks, *"Who do the people say the Son of Man is?"* Interestingly, the popular rumors only name dead saints of the past. Maybe Jesus is John the Baptist with a new head, Elijah, Jeremiah or one of the prophets. This is significant: when Jesus was on the earth, there was no one like him—no other living soul could compare. No one thought Jesus was like King Herod or the High Priest or their favorite Pharisee. Such was his greatness that it was easier to imagine someone rising from the dead than it was to compare him to any other person alive. Jesus doesn't end the conversation with this general question. He gets personal as they stand among the idol statues of Caesarea Philippi. "But who do you say that I am?"

There's so much to this question! There's word play; I Am is Yahweh, the Hebrew name for God, as if Jesus is giving them a hint in the way he phrases the question. And then there's all the choices. They could pick one of the popular theories, John the Baptist or Elijah. They could look around and pick a god like Zeus or Hermes. But Peter, moved by the Spirit proclaims, *"You are the Christ (anointed one), the Son of the living God."* How profound and perfect a proclamation! In a sea of dead god statues he calls Jesus, the Son of the *Living God*, the Son of the Great I AM. There's a stark contrast drawn—all the other "gods" and all the people that you could compare Jesus to have one thing in common—they're dead! But Jesus is alive!

Jesus replies by calling Peter by his first and last name, Bar-Jonah meaning son of Jonah. It's as if Jesus is saying, you call me by my name Jesus Bar-Yahweh, Son of the Living God, and I'll call you by yours. And then, standing before the "Gate of Hades" at what was believed to be the cave to the underworld, Jesus declares that not even the gates of hell can prevail against the church of Jesus Christ that Peter now holds the keys to because of his faith and confession.

Our temptation today is to make our conversations about Jesus in the past tense. We talk about who Jesus was instead of who Jesus is. The whole point of this conversation was that Jesus is alive and his Father is alive. This hasn't changed. He's still different from all the other gods and people that we could compare him to. Moreover, it could be said that since Jesus is the firstborn from among the dead, he's more alive now than ever. (Romans 8) This week we'll look at who Jesus was when he was on the earth and what that means for us who have his living presence with us always through the Holy Spirit. (Matthew 28:20) But today we need to start by remembering that our God is not the great I WAS but the great I AM. He is with us. He is present. And as we go on the mission in our hometowns, the historical Jesus may have some impact, but if you really want to reach the lost all around you, show them that your savior IS the Son of the Living God by showing them how alive he is in you!

Apply

People still say all kinds of things about who they think Jesus is. What are some of the opinions you have heard? When you think about Jesus in the gospels what characteristics do you admire? How could those characteristics come alive in you through the living presence of Jesus?

Do

Pray through a gospel by reading through the subheadings and thinking about who Jesus was. Ask God to show you how Jesus is alive and powerful in your life today. Set an alarm on your phone to remind you throughout the day that Jesus is with you.

Pray through the people on your Prayer Banner and get ready to intentionally begin sharing your faith and the gospel with them.

Yield

Lord, help me to see how Jesus is alive in me today...

Tuesday: Jesus Makes Us Strong

Read
Mark 1:21-28
Acts 4:5-22

Examine

Jesus was strong. If you spent a day with him you'd be amazed at all the ways he was strong. He was physically strong. He was a builder with stone and wood and ancient tools. He made a whip and overturned tables (not the lightweight Ikea stuff). He eventually endured the whip himself before enduring the cross. But Jesus' strength went beyond his physical ability.

He was also resilient. He had the strength of character to persevere through hard things. His ministry was one fight after another. With Pharisees, with demons, even with his own disciples. He had to make resolute decisions and stick with them. He had to fight to stay close to the Father. He was certainly resilient but his strength even went beyond that!

People were impressed by his power, the authority with which he taught, spoke and commanded. It was power they had never seen before. Something new. He didn't ask for permission or apologize as he spoke. The crowds stood in awe, amazed at the strength with which he taught.

Throughout his life, Jesus' disciples often showed the exact opposite characteristics. They were impressively *weak*. Physically they couldn't stay awake. Their resilience was challenged by the slightest opposition. And they lacked authority even though Jesus had given it to them. But something changed after the resurrection. These same men, now filled with the Holy Spirit, the living presence of Jesus, boldly preach the gospel and baptize 3,000 in one day. They are challenged to stop speaking by the religious leaders who are amazed by their boldness and strength. They even endure the whip. When they see the disciples, the religious leaders are reminded of Jesus, who in their minds is dead. Just as they had with Jesus, the only explanation for the disciples power that they can see is that someone must have risen from the dead—only this time they are right! The people with the presence of Jesus have been made strong because of him and the crowds are reacting the same way they did when Jesus was physically among them. Jesus made them strong.

Apply

Jesus made the first disciples strong and his presence makes us strong. How does the Holy Spirit make you strong, resilient, or powerful? Are there areas in your life that you've been weak? How could relying on Jesus' presence today make you strong?

Do

This may seem silly but look in the mirror and flex. It doesn't matter how strong or in shape you think you are. As you look at your power pose in the mirror tell yourself, "Jesus makes me strong." That's it. Just do that and then go about your day as his disciple.

Add a person from your Prayer List to your Share List that will require you to be strong. Ask God for the strength to share with that person at the next Spirit initiated opportunity.

Yield

Lord, make me strong so I can share my faith with...

Wednesday: Jesus Makes Us Wise _____

Read

Luke 2:41-52
Luke 20:1-7, 26, 40
Acts 26:1-32

Examine

Jesus was wise. Even at a young age he impressed the teachers with his wisdom. During his ministry he was so wise that he shut down arguments, answering questions with better questions and silencing the brightest minds of his day.

With the outpouring of the Holy Spirit his disciples became wise too. Paul's wisdom was so evident that powerful people questioned if he wasn't so smart that he was losing his mind. I guess he was crazy smart!

So often, we fail to share about Jesus because we don't feel like we know enough. Paul believed that disciples of Jesus are filled with knowledge and able to instruct (Romans 15:14). In Corinth, he actually decided to purposely come across as unwise so people would be impressed by the presence of Jesus and not by some super smart Christian (1 Corinthians 2:1-5). While we should study and pray so we can become more wise, we shouldn't use a lack of knowledge or experience as an excuse to keep us on the sidelines of evangelism. The truth is, no one is wise compared to Jesus. We need him to make us wise in every moment so we can share the gospel with his power and wisdom instead of our own, no matter how experienced we may become.

Because Jesus lives in you, you can share your faith with anybody. The apostles even shared with kings and rulers. He makes us super-naturally wise when we share our faith. Not sharing with people because they intimidate us or we feel uncertain about how to help them is like a hero not using a superpower. This super-powered wisdom can only be unleashed when we build up the courage and reliance on Jesus to share our faith and watch him work.

Apply

Are there people that you have not shared with because you don't think you know how? How could Jesus make you wise so you can share with that person? What could you study on their behalf? Who could you seek advice from that may have the wisdom you need?

Do

Add a person from your Prayer List to your Share List that you feel inadequate to share with. If there is anyone you haven't shared with because of a lack of wisdom, pray for wisdom and write down what you will do to be more wise for them *and* **to rely on Jesus and share your faith, anyway.** Jesus makes us wise!

Yield

Lord, make me wise so I can share with...

Thursday: Jesus Makes Us Creative _____

Read

Mark 4:1-34
Acts 17:16-34

Examine

Jesus was creative. John 1, Colossians 1 and Hebrews 1 each tell us that all things were created through him. That's pretty creative! (Understatement of the year, century, eternity). His parables are an amazing example of his creativity displayed as he walked in the midst of his creation. He saw God in the things of everyday life and in doing so made his stories about God relevant for all time. The parables also put the onus on the listener to be creative as well. In order to respond to Jesus, a listener would have to ponder the symbolism of the parable so that only those who were truly seeking God could understand the meaning.

The Sermon on the Mount is a prime example of Jesus' creativity. I remember being on a hillside by the Sea of Galilee and hearing Matthew 5-7 read aloud. As I looked out at the landscape, the wildflowers and the sea, it was as if Jesus was in my head keeping my attention on his words by inserting whatever I was looking at into his sermon!

The presence of Jesus allowed those who would follow Jesus to be creative too. Paul's message in Athens is an amazing example of creativity. As Paul walked through Athens, the Spirit showed him an idol to an unknown god. Paul knew exactly how to address some of the wisest people in the world—he'd tell them who that unknown god was! They were captivated!

The presence of Jesus makes us creative too. Relying on the creator to share our faith creatively is so important. It makes evangelism personal and special. Like Jesus' parables and Paul's speech, creativity can cause people to see God in a whole new way. What an amazing privilege to see Jesus' creativity change someone's outlook on God as he works in us and through us.

Apply

You may not feel like a very creative or artistic person but Jesus makes us creative. How could a creative approach to sharing your faith make a difference with a stubborn or stuck person?

Do

Add a person from your Prayer List to your Share List that you could creatively share with. Choose one person that you've been praying for and think about a way to creatively invite them to church, an event or a Bible study. Ask God to help you create an opportunity for the Spirit to work in a special way.

Yield

Creator, make me creative so I can share with...

Friday: Jesus Makes Us Honest _____

Read

John 8:30-59
Acts 6:8-7:2, 7:51-53 (Read his whole speech in chapter 7 if time allows)

Examine

Jesus was honest. In today's passage his honesty almost got him killed. Eventually it does get him killed. The faithful who followed him were made honest by his presence in the lives. Stephen's speech is an amazing retelling of Israel's history that sets up his audience for some brutal honesty at the end. They keep killing the prophets (and missing the point entirely, they kill Stephen).

Sometimes we pray and wonder and waffle about what to say and when to speak up and struggle to get just the right words to share our faith. I've had people in my life that I'd shared with 100 times in my head but never actually spoke up because I didn't know how to say what needed to be said. Sometimes what people need most is just a good dose of honesty. This isn't a license to be harsh or insensitive but an invitation to have tough *and* loving conversations with the people we care about.

Sometimes people need to know that they aren't living in a way that ends with them spending eternity with God. We have NO authority to make that call or to tell people that they are going to hell (that's God's job on the last day) but we can lovingly and honestly talk this through with people and help them come to the conclusion themselves. Honesty: If someone is experiencing hell on earth—loneliness, separation from God, rebellion, despair, etc—they are setting themselves up perfectly for hell in the next life. Ouch! But one painful conversation like this about matters of life and death might just be the spark that keeps your friend from pain that lasts forever.

Jesus makes us honest and uses our imperfect honesty to show the perfect truth of his nature to those who so desperately need it if we let him live powerfully in us.

Apply

Is there someone in your life that you just need to be honest with? How could you have a life changing and possibly life saving conversation with someone on your prayer list? What fears do you have about being lovingly honest?

Do

Add a person from your Prayer List to your Share List that you need to be honest with. Decide to be honest and start praying for an opportunity to be real with your friend or family member. Start looking for scriptures so that Jesus' truth and love will shine through your conversation.

Yield

Lord, give me the honest words I need to lovingly share with...

Saturday: Jesus Makes Us Urgent _____

Read

Mark 1:16-20
Acts 8:26-40

Examine

Jesus was urgent. When he called, he expected an immediate response (Luke 9:57-63). Think about the impact he had in a ministry that lasted only a few years. He had to be urgent and expect the surrounding people to act decisively whether they accepted him or rejected him.

Urgency breeds more urgency, just as a lack of urgency breeds complacency. The Spirit worked in the early church to spread the gospel to the far reaches of the Roman Empire and beyond in just a few decades. When people heard the gospel and responded with repentance and faith, they were baptized right away. They lived like they really believed that Jesus was active among them, changing lives and saving souls.

If we lack urgency, it speaks volumes about what we truly believe. If Jesus is really living in you, then you should imitate his urgency to see souls saved. In fact, one of the reasons he is alive in you is so he can work urgently in your life to help the surrounding people to know him.

Jesus makes us urgent. A few years ago we had students come from other campus ministries to help us build a campus ministry for just 3 weeks. They knew they had limited time, so they shared with great urgency, holding Bible studies daily instead of weekly. In the months after they left, a ministry was born by their fruit. Amazingly, the first disciples in that ministry shared in their urgency even though they had more time to share their faith.

Apply

What does your urgency (or lack of urgency) to share your faith say about your faith? Nobody knows how much time they have for themselves or the people around them. What if you shared the gospel with this reality in mind?

Do

Add a person from your **Prayer List** to your **Share List** that urgently needs to hear about Jesus. Is there someone who sticks out more than the others as needing to see Jesus right away? Write down how you will share urgently with this person that you love.

Yield

Lord, make me urgent so I can share as soon as possible with...

Section 2: Feet

"Go home to your friends and tell them how much the Lord has done for you, and how he has had mercy on you."

—Mark 5:19

In the last chapter we met Legion, the man whom Jesus healed of many demons. You'd think this guy would definitely be someone that Jesus would have welcomed as a follower. He even asks to go with Jesus after he is freed. Can you imagine the success Jesus could have had in his travelling ministry by parading a completely healed demoniac around with him wherever he went? But Jesus, always thinking on another level, rejects his request to become a follower and instead sends him back to his hometown which happens to be an area consisting of ten cities.

Go to your hometown. That's where the title of this book came from. If you've been freed from your demons and sins by Jesus and decided to follow him, then you've got to get up on your feet and go into your city, town, village, unincorporated township or wherever it is you live and tell the people "how he has had mercy on you." You are living in your mission field and it's time to lose your seat and move your feet. As it is written, *"How beautiful are the feet of those who preach the good news!"* (Romans 10:15).

In the next four weeks the challenges are going to ramp up and the faith you gained last month will be called upon for action. People aren't going to come up to us and ask us to help them become followers of Jesus. We're going to go to them!

Week 5: Heroes of the Faith— Old Testament

"When you go out to war against your enemies, and see horses and chariots and an army larger than your own, you shall not be afraid of them, for the Lord your God is with you..."

—Deuteronomy 20:1

Read Deuteronomy 20:1-9

In Deuteronomy 20, instructions are given in the law for when Israel goes to war. War is a reality. It's something that people have always needed to prepare for. It's also a spiritual reality that we should prepare for as kingdom people.

Can you imagine this scene? Israel is lined up for battle and across the battlefield is a much larger army. A priest comes out in front of the army with his high hat and colorful breastplate and reminds you that though their army may look larger, you've got the Lord himself fighting with you. Do not be afraid. God goes ahead of you and he gives the victory.

Then the officers come in and follow up the priest's speech. They ask if there's anyone with a new house or a new wife. If you've got something that you really want to stay alive for then you can go home to it. Moreover, anyone who is afraid may also leave.

So, your army is already smaller than the enemy and now people are filing out the back and leaving the battlefield. At the onset this must have been discouraging. Can you imagine the downcast faces of the afraid shuffling by? But then the people who are left tighten up their ranks. Think about the result: You know that the person fighting on your left and the person fighting on your right are all in. They aren't dreaming of home. They are focused on the battle. They aren't overcome by fear.

> **God's instructions for war create a fierce group of warriors that he can lead into battle.**

And the priests words remain true. It doesn't matter how many remain to fight anyway because God himself is leading the charge.

It all starts with the word "When". War is not optional or even avoidable for God's people. War is an eventuality. It should not surprise us then, as the New Israel, that we've been commissioned by Jesus. We studied the Great Commission last week. Commission is a military word.

When Paul wrote about the Christian life in his letter to the Ephesians, he wrote about war. *"For our struggle is not against flesh and blood, but against the rulers, against the authorities, against the powers of this dark world and against the spiritual forces of evil in the heavenly realms."* That's New Testament (Ephesians 6:12) and it's talking about war. Paul goes on to describe the armor that we are to take with us into battle. This makes all those Old Testament stories about battles and heroes more than just entertaining reading. Those texts can train us for spiritual warfare. Let's breakdown one of the greatest battles in the Old Testament and see what we can take from the battle of Ai (Ayee) and apply to Jesus' war for the souls of men.

Go ahead and read about the battle in Joshua 5:13-8:29. What an action packed passage!

Joshua 5:13-15

Whose Side Are You Fighting On?

Before we get to Ai, we've (literally) got to go through Jericho and its mighty walls. Joshua is restless before the battle. He sneaks close to Jericho for one last look. He is startled by a "man" with a drawn sword and he asks what seems like a good question if you were in Joshua's shoes. "Are you fighting for us or our enemies?" Tell me whose side are you fighting on? It's a logical question but you know it's the wrong question because the man with the sword answers the either/or question by saying "No." Neither option applies. Turns out this isn't a man at all, it's the commander of the Lord's army. So, how much should we expect this life in Christ to be a fight? Well, God's got an army!

People debate about who this commander is. Is it an angel or archangel? I think it's the pre-incarnate Jesus Christ himself. Here are a few reasons why: First,

Joshua (same name as Jesus) falls on his face in worship and the man does not tell him to stand up and worship God only. When John does this (twice) in Revelation the angels are quick to correct him. Second, the ground that the man is standing on is holy ground just as the ground around the burning bush from which God himself spoke was holy ground. And third, when Jesus is arrested he tells his disciples to put away their swords because he could call on his Father and *"he will at once send me more than 12 legions of angels"* (Matthew 26:54). Kind of sounds like Jesus is saying that he's the commander of the Lord's army!

What we do and think before the battle is just as important as the battle itself. As we prepare to obey Jesus, our commissioning officer, mustering up the faith to share the gospel, we would be wise to consider Joshua's question and Jesus' answer. We want God to take sides. Our side, to be specific. But God doesn't take sides. We take his side and he leads us into battle. God isn't fighting for us. We're fighting for him. He's in charge and he's already won.

> *Even when all seemed lost at Gethsemane and the disciples sheathed their swords and watched Jesus get taken away to be crucified, the commander of the Lord's army was winning the battle with the greatest "rope-a-dope" of all time. Three days later when he left that tomb empty the war was won.*

We can get into this habit when we pray of telling God OUR battle plans and making demands of what we want. We get these ideas about how people are supposed to respond when we share our faith. And then we get disappointed. *The battle before the battle is surrender to the one who is truly in charge.* The commander of the Lord's army has sent us out on a mission to go and make disciples. He hasn't given us all the details and he hasn't said it would be easy. So we go, and we trust him to lead us into battle. This week's challenge keeps this in mind and it's SUCH AN ADVENTURE!

People Aren't The Enemy, They're The Mission

Israel goes into battle at Jericho. But God's in control so it looks nothing like a battle. Instead of fighting, they march and blow trumpets for 7 days and then they all scream and the walls of Jericho come tumbling down (Not the battle plan I would have come up with!). Achan infamously disobeys and hides some spoils of war but God's people move on to the next battle, the first battle of Ai, not knowing of Achan's sin.

Joshua 7:1-5

They end up fighting God. That's what happens when you try to win souls but your own soul is riddled with hidden sin or willful rebellion against God. I'm sure you want to be involved in saving some souls, but if you're hiding sin, you and your church would be better off if you started with your own! Let's get open this week. Put the book down, pick up your phone and get ahold of someone you trust so you can confess. *Your whole church will benefit more from sharing one unconfessed sin than from sharing your faith 100 times with sin hidden in your life!*

Joshua 8:1

There must have been some fear among Joshua and the Israelites even after dealing with the sin that was holding them back. They had the first rout that Ai dealt them fresh in their minds. So God starts the battle plan by saying, *"Do not fear."* Then he lets Joshua know that he has given Ai into his hand. The battle is already decided.

One of the biggest things that keeps us from boldly sharing our faith is fear. And this fear is not irrational. We can each provide great detail about our own personal Ai's. Times when we confidently shared our faith, but we were beaten back, forced to retreat, embarrassed.

Can you think of scars and battle wounds in your past?
- Maybe your Ai is someone who studied the Bible and almost made Jesus Lord but at the last minute couldn't commit. Or someone who got baptized but quickly fell away.
- Maybe your Ai is a loved one who you've lovingly gone to battle for time and again but their hearts are just not ready.
- Maybe your Ai is on campus, you were sharing your faith and you got rejected and felt embarrassed.

When this happens we can start to see the battle for people's souls as a fight against the people themselves. It's so crucial for us to remember that we are fighting for these people—never against them. **They're the mission. Never the enemy.**

Standing God's Ground, Not Conquering New Territory

Ephesians 6:10-13

Do you see who the real enemy is? It's a bigger threat than your atheist co-worker or professor. It's the darkness itself. Not the people. But there's good news here.

In many ways the end of Ephesians is like the Deuteronomy 20 of the New Testament. This is our summons to war. But something has changed in the New Testament. We're still at war. But we're no longer going out and conquering. Jesus, the commander of the Lord's army, has won the war by sacrificing himself for God's kingdom. His resurrection means there's nothing left to conquer. Satan, sin and death have been defeated—there's no territory that isn't ruled by God.

But the battle rages on because people don't recognize God's kingdom. They're stuck in rebellious self-rule. *This makes every day before Jesus comes back special.* Each day is an opportunity to win souls for Christ in his kingdom. Interestingly, we are not told to conquer. We are told to stand and to stand firm. This is God's territory. Jesus won it. So even as we "go and make" we're not invading. We're just holding on to what is already God's. Our mission is to show people that they can stop fighting (surrender) and recognize this truth: Jesus is Lord—that's the good news or gospel—Jesus is King.

What an amazing mission!

Are you ready? You've learned in the last four weeks about God's heart—how he loves every soul. You've learned about the power of prayer and you're praying —don't slow down! You've seen the gospel and its power to save. And you've been assured that Jesus goes with us on the mission with all of his power. Are you ready to go out into God's territory and join in the mission of the saints? It's time.

Being Heroic

But first, let's look at what happened in the 2nd battle of Ai. The sin that was holding them back was removed and Joshua is getting his battle plans directly from the Lord. They send the army just as before and the men of Ai are winning again. Israel retreats just like the first time and all the people of Ai rush out thinking they've won as they did the last time. But they soon look back and see that their city is on fire. It was a fake retreat to lure them out of their city. Israel had 5000 troops waiting to ambush them. The smoke signals the bulk of Joshua's army to stop its fake retreat and to turn and fight. The ambushing soldiers join the fight and the people of Ai are surrounded and defeated.

I love imagining this battle—it's so epic and it's in the Bible! Take a moment and read Joshua 8:18 again. Can you imagine Joshua fighting with a javelin? He stretches it out and the whole army moves as he stands in a power pose. Epic. Joshua is an amazing warrior and a heroic leader.

Our Bible is filled with hero stories like this one. It's littered with true tales of men and women who fought alongside God to do seemingly impossible things. We might think that the days of being heroic are over or that they're just stories. But, when we decide to fight for souls God raises up a new generation of heroes. Think about the person or people who shared Jesus with you. We all have spiritual heroes and heroines who helped us come to God or kept us from leaving God or inspired us in some way. Just as the spiritual battle isn't just an Old Testament thing, being heroic by the power of God is something we can experience in our lives today. I like to watch sports. It's inspiring. It's the only thing that can make me cry. But I'd always choose to play a sport myself over watching one. In Christ, we are not just relegated to reading about the heroes of old—we get to be heroes now. Or as Jesus himself put it, "I say to you, whoever believes in me will also do the works that I do; and greater works than these will he do, because I am going to the Father" (John 14:12).

This week's devotionals are all about looking at Old Testament heroes and learning how we can be heroic today. It's time to share your faith with as many types of people as possible this week and inspire others by putting it on your Mission Map. You're going to see how much impact God can have through you as you stand firm for the Lord all over your hometown. This is fun stuff—this is the great Christian adventure. This is your chance to be a hero for someone else through the power and love of Jesus Christ.

Week 5: In the Field Training

Peek at the Week
The time has come! Get out there and share your faith!

Old Testament Scavangelism Challenge
How many of the 21 people on the list can you share with?

- Every time you share, place a **mission memo** on your **mission map!**
- Take time to write down possible people or places so you can pray first.

I'll admit these are pretty "Punny" so have fun with it! If you don't understand a reference look the person up! #HometownMissionary #Scavangelism are the hashtags you can use to share about who you're sharing with!

- ❏ Goliath - Share with someone who intimidates you
- ❏ Armor Bearer - Share while you're hanging out with another Christian
- ❏ Moses - Share with a Boss/Coach or Leader
- ❏ Witch of Endor - Share with the Last Person You'd Expect to be Open
- ❏ Abraham - Someone Who Recently Moved
- ❏ Gideon - Someone Wearing Fleece
- ❏ Elisha - A Bald or Balding Person (Be nice and watch for bears!)
- ❏ Samson - Long Hair or Big Muscles (or both!)
- ❏ Asahel - Someone on a Run or at the Gym
- ❏ Ehud - A Left-Handed Person
- ❏ Hannah - Someone who looks sad
- ❏ Ezra - Someone Reading
- ❏ Esau - A Redhead or Someone Eating Soup
- ❏ Joseph - Someone with Bright Colored Clothing
- ❏ Sarah - Someone Who's Laughing
- ❏ Rachel - At the Water Cooler or Coffee Bar
- ❏ Nehemiah - Someone Short
- ❏ Eve - Someone Eating a Snack
- ❏ Shadrach, Meshach and Abednego—Share with a Group of 3 People
- ❏ David - Share with Someone Ruddy and Handsome
- ❏ Jezebel - Share with Someone Wearing Makeup

It may sound strange to think of people in the Old Testament sharing their faith. But this week we'll see examples of evangelism heroes and let them inspire us to share our faith in a crazy creative way. "Scavangelism" or Scavenger Hunt Evangelism is a fun way to be bold and let the Spirit use you to meet new people or minister to people you already know but haven't talked to about your faith. This week we really start sharing our faith! Be bold! Be heroic! Have fun—sharing about Jesus is the greatest adventure in Christianity!

A Challenging Family Devotional

- Go to a park and have a picnic or go out to an informal place to eat.
- Have a hero discussion with your kids and talk about the people in your life that God used to bring you to God.
- Ask them about their spiritual heroes.
- Share about your spiritual heroes this week on social media with the hashtags #FaithHero #HometownMissionary.
- After your discussion go share your faith as a family using the Scavangelism sheet!

Monday: Worship on the Way

Read

Genesis 12:1-9
Genesis 13:14-18
Genesis 14:17-20

Examine

You may have noticed in today's reading that everywhere Abraham went he built an altar to worship God. After fighting to get his nephew Lot freed from marauders, he ends up worshipping Melchizedek, the king of peace and righteousness. This priestly king comes out of nowhere as a figure that the writer of Hebrews clearly connects to Christ himself. Abraham even tithes to him. It's as if Abraham was so in tune with worshipping everywhere he went that God brought a full Church service to him thousands of years before Jesus and the church! It's as if the New Testament breaks out way back in Genesis 14.

Our lives can be so compartmentalized. Sometimes it's almost like we have different versions of ourselves. There's a church version, a work version and a home version. What amazes me about Abraham is that he was his faithful, God loving, altar building self everywhere he went (except maybe when he was around kings who took a liking to his wife!).

What if we took our worship with us after church on Sunday morning or even after our daily devotional times and prayers? What if there was only one version of you? The God loving, Jesus following, joy filled version!

Interestingly, even without a home country or children (at the time), Abraham's wealth and household grew. Because he worshipped everywhere he went, God blessed him everywhere he went. We tend to see evangelism as a thing we do sometimes maybe if there's a church focus on it. If we worship God everywhere we go as disciples of Jesus 24/7, I don't think we'd ever need to hear a lesson on evangelism again! God blesses unity. Sometimes we even lack unity in ourselves— we lack congruence. How much would your church grow if you decided to worship everywhere you went? What if sharing your faith stopped being an add on religious activity and became a regular part of your life in Christ?

Apply

Pray and write out the ways you are different at church, home, work, and in recreation or leisure time. How could you be a worshipper in all of those places? How could you make each place a place where God is honored (an altar)?

Do

Get ready for work like you get ready for church (or like you should get ready for church): Think about who you will encourage and how you can be a joyful presence at your job. Is there anyone you could share your faith with? **On the way home from work think about what your family needs. How can you bring God into your home?**

Yield

I will worship you with my life wherever I go today...

Tuesday: No More Grasshoppers _____

Read

Numbers 13

Examine

It's not just sharing your faith that counts, but how you share your faith makes a big difference. If we share our faith but don't really believe that God is working in the lives of those we're sharing with and making them open, then do we really have faith to share? If we just share because of a church focus or a feeling of obligation or even this book, are we really sharing our faith? If we share about Jesus but lack enthusiasm and zeal should we expect anyone to respond to our lack of faith with faith? (Amazingly, sometimes people do respond even when our hearts are off because God is working! See Philippians 1:15-18).

In today's chapter, you can see the difference that faith makes. Caleb and Joshua see the exact same cities and people as the other spies but they come to radically different conclusions about what is possible. Faith makes the difference. If we share our faith but really don't believe that there's any hope that a person might say yes, then we need to check our faith. It's interesting that the ten faithless spies said, *"we seemed to ourselves like grasshoppers, and so we seemed to them."* How did they know that? They projected their lack of faith onto those outside of the kingdom instead of digging deep and finding God in a situation that looked difficult.

Joshua and Caleb were so faithful that I don't think it mattered how tall the enemy was or how thick their walls were. They believed that God could do anything! And they were right! They were thinking about how big those grapes were and not how big of a task taking the Promised Land would be. And after all, it was called the Promised Land for a reason—God promised it! Just like Jesus has promised to be with us always as we share our faith.

Apply

What if you focused more on God and less on the person you are sharing your faith with? Think about the excitement and zeal with which you share your faith. Would you say yes to someone who invited you to church or a Bible study with the faith and enthusiasm that you have?

Do

Share your faith today. Think about God and honoring him and all the work he's put into this person you are sharing with. Smile, be joyful and excited—you're offering salvation through the power of the gospel. Use the scavangelism sheet if it helps you.

Yield

Lord help me see with eyes of faith as I share my faith today...

Wednesday: Toppling Giants

Read
1 Samuel 17 (Read aloud if possible)

Examine
This is one of the most familiar stories in the Bible but I wonder if you've ever looked at it through the eyes of evangelism? David is sharing his faith, toppling giants and inspiring God's people!

Just as we saw Melchizedek in Monday's reading as a type of Christ, Goliath is a type of Satan. He's opposing God and accusing God's people day after day. Israel trembles in fear at the sound of his voice and the sight of his oversized armor and spear.

Enter the shepherd boy, David: He's doubted by his own brothers. Have you ever felt discouragement and doubt because of your family? David doesn't let his family's opinions keep him from sharing his faith. He doesn't abandon them but he simply turns to speak to others who might be willing to hear what he has to say.

Next, he's doubted by the king. But then he shares his faith with Saul (who had none). He tells Saul that all the things in his life have led to this moment. He wasn't just protecting his flock from bears and wolves. He was being trained by God to topple giants. David is sharing his testimony with King Saul, who was quite tall himself. In a sense, Saul was the first giant that David had to topple. David's God story is so powerful that Saul even tries to give David his armor. He was able to expand Saul's view of what God was doing—he really shared his faith!

Last, David faces Goliath. Before any stones fly from his sling, there is a verbal attack from the mocking giant that is countered with one of the most heroic and faithful paragraphs in the Bible. David knows that God is fighting this battle and that God will be honored. "The battle is the Lord's."

Apply
Who are the giants in your life? Maybe your family is a giant discouragement? Maybe you have a friend or co-worker that you really look up to? Fear can keep us from sharing our faith with such people. But our giants need God too! Write down some people you consider giants on your prayer banner and pray for them.

Do
Share your faith with a giant in your life. If you don't know how, pray about it and

learn from David's example. (No, don't hit them in the head with rocks or threaten to feed their bodies to birds). I can't tell you exactly what to say but I believe what you say probably doesn't matter as much as you think. David shows us that what matters most is that we care about honoring our great big God more than fearing the reaction of the giants in our lives. Check off the Goliath challenge on the scavangelism page.

Yield

Lord I have this giant in my life...Give me the words to say and the faith to share so my giant can meet you...

Thursday: Fire Bones _____

Read

Jeremiah 1:4-19
Jeremiah 20:9

Examine

What's in your bones? Jeremiah was called by God to share the word. We have been called by God to share the word. God makes it clear to Jeremiah that his message should not be discouraged or altered by the people's response. People will be stubborn and hard-hearted, God's word is not affected by people. Unless of course, God's people are affected by the hard hearted and stubborn.

It's not about people's response. It's about how we respond when people aren't open. Are we faithful that God is working through the Spirit and it's just not the right time for that person yet or do we lose faith? It comes down to what's in our bones.

Jeremiah famously claims that if he stopped sharing his faith, it would be like a fire shut up in his bones. It would wear him out to not talk about God. The burden would be too great. I'll ask again, what's in your bones?

If our bones, our core conviction, isn't about God and salvation and saving those who would spend eternity without God then we've got to work on our core convictions. Something about salvation may be missing from our hearts if we don't feel the pain of the lost in our bones. Has the fire gone out in your bones?

The only way to get the fire back is to get God inside of you. Put his word in your bones. Spend time with other people who love God. Ask God to fill you. You need this—but so do the people that God has put in your life. Your fire, the content of your bones, is their hope for God. We need God and we need to get fired up!

Apply

Are you lacking zeal and enthusiasm for God and the mission? What's missing? Is it devotional times, discouragement, faithlessness? Whatever it is God can make you into a strong pillar if you'll decide to rely on him.

Do

Take a day off from sharing your faith and fill up your bones with God. **Read, pray, worship and fall in love with God today so that you can't help but share your faith tomorrow.**

Yield

Lord, fill my bones with Spirit fire...

Friday: See My Zeal For The Lord

Read

2 Kings 9:14-37
2 Kings 10:15-17
Jeremiah 35

Examine

Jehu was a radical dude! At one point during his rampage he picks up a man named Jehonadab the son of Rechab and takes him on a chariot ride. Over a century later in the book of Jeremiah we learn that Rechab's descendants are some of the only righteous people in all of Israel. Ever since that chariot ride they've lived in tents (intense!) and abstained from wine—content to be wanderers who served God even though they were not considered true Israelites.

We underestimate the power of a good talk. Jesus shared his faith in John 1 by simply spending a day with Andrew and Simon (Peter). I can see the crazy in Jehu's eyes when he reaches out his hand to Jehonadab and says, "Come with me and see my zeal for the Lord." When he stepped on that Chariot his life was changed as were the lives of his children and grandchildren. When we share Jesus, we never know just how lasting and powerful our impact will be!

Can people see your zeal? Are you jealous for God? How would someone be affected by God if they spent a day with you? Are you willing to give someone who is seeking God a day or an evening of your time? Most people go their whole lives without seeing a person who is really in love with God—you could be the exception to this and the eternal difference!

Apply

Think about how your life was changed by someone's willingness to talk about Jesus with you. Dream about having generational impact by spending time with people who are willing to seek God.

Do

Have a good talk about Jesus with someone you love. Spend time doing what matters most: Sharing how amazing Jesus is. Let your zeal for God shine.

Yield

Lord, use one small conversation about Jesus today to have an impact beyond what I will ever know...

Saturday: Prepare The Way

Read

Luke 3

Examine

Even though John the Baptist's story occurs in the New Testament, his life and death occur under the old promise. We can learn so much from the last of the prophets and the forerunner of Christ.

John goes to the Jordan; the same river Israel crossed to enter the promised land. He is asking people to stop relying on their heritage and ancestry as God's people who crossed the Jordan. He wants them to cross the Jordan again through baptism and identify with the new thing God will be doing through Jesus Christ. Many come to him to repent of relying on their heritage instead of the living God.

Interestingly, he does not call on people to quit life in order to repent. Instead he calls them to inject God into all the part of their lives. When the crowds ask, *"What then shall we do?"* (just as they will ask of Peter in Acts 2), he tells the rich to be generous, the tax collectors to be honest, and the soldiers to not abuse their authority. In other words, in whatever you do, be righteous and follow God.

We still fall for the false dichotomy that following God means quitting the world and living in a hole in the ground. Quite the opposite, following God means injecting God into all the things of the world that we do. Today, the need is so great for Christians to live in the world and still remain fully alive for Christ. I can think of no bigger need than with our children's activities. **The reason your child is in soccer, volleyball, chess or girl scouts is for you to bring the kingdom to the parents**

and children in that group. John shows us in his teaching to the people at the Jordan—there is a way to be righteous no matter what you are doing.

Apply

Why do you have the interests and hobbies that you have? Why are your children involved in the activities that they are involved in? The ONLY reason is so you can meet other parents and share the gospel. Anything else is icing on the cake.

Do

Make a plan to share with people as you enjoy your hobbies or your kid's extra-curricular activities. Inject God into every part of your life and see how he wants to use YOU to advance his kingdom.

Yield

Father, show me how I can bring your son into all the activities that I and my family participate in...

Week 6: The Art of Hospitality

"Let brotherly love continue. Do not neglect to show hospitality to strangers, for thereby some have entertained angels unawares."
—Hebrews 13:1-2

Are you busy? Are you important? Doing important things? Do you have boundaries in place to protect yourself, your family and your schedule? This chapter is for you!

We set up boundaries to protect ourselves and our families: schedule boundaries, people boundaries, boundaries about how open we will be with our lives (pride boundaries). None of that is wrong in and of itself. To an extent all of those things are necessary. But our attitudes and boundaries can become sin and end up hurting ourselves and our families instead of protecting us.

> *There's an antidote to all of this! There's a way to have boundaries but not be controlled by our boundaries—boundaries become idols—**the antidote is hospitality.***

Hospitality: intentionally showing kindness to others by **letting people in**, shakes us out of our comfort zones and pushes our boundaries. Without regular and intentional hospitality to brothers and sisters in church, neighbors, co-workers, classmates, and even strangers, we will become defined by the boundaries we set for ourselves instead of letting God push those boundaries into places of adventure and impact.

This only gets more challenging as we get more to protect. More money, more responsibility, a spouse, children, homes, hobbies; we think that the more we have the more we give. But the statistics tell us that the more we have the more we seek to protect what we have and to keep ourselves from losing the things, people and values that we believe we earned.

Our faith goes on defense—prevent defense—and we're not about adventure and impact anymore. We're about defending. We've all seen Christians like this and we've probably all been Christians like this; more interested in not losing what we have than taking the risk of going and making disciples as we've been commissioned to do. As a Detroit Lions fan when I hear the announcer say that they're in the lead and in a prevent defense I shudder! I've seen time and again how over-focusing on prevention brings loss.

Our boundaries, taking care of and protecting the things God has given us are good, as long as we don't become fully devoted to protecting and preventing. We may think hospitality is no big deal, but it's amazing how an intentional, proactive offense against the prevention mindset can change everything. Hospitality is our offense, and therefore, a grace filled gift from God!

Hebrews 13:1-2

This is one of the most intriguing scriptures in the Bible. We can't help but wonder when we read it if we have entertained angels unawares? And this mystery centers on hospitality.

In the classic Christmas movie *It's a Wonderful Life* it is famously stated that every time a bell rings an angel gets its wings. When I saw that as a kid it made me want to ring as many bells as possible. Let's get those angels their wings! Now as I look at the scriptures, I see that it may truly be possible to get angels their "wings". Did you know that when we practice hospitality we might just be making angels? I'll explain by taking a deep dive into Genesis 18, a chapter in which Abraham shows hospitality and actually entertains angels.

Genesis 18:1-22—Read it!

Before we get into the deep waters of this passage, I want to share Abraham and Sarah's experience and demonstrate some practical points about hospitality:

Hospitality isn't going to be convenient. If it was everybody would do it. It's hot, Abraham didn't have this meeting in his calendar. These three men just show up on his front porch. Abraham has worshipped God all over the promised land and had many conversations with God so he knows that these aren't just three dudes walking in the desert. This is God. This is the pre-incarnate Jesus. Remember the meeting with Joshua last week? Maybe he's with two angels or this is the trinity itself in some form?

We get nervous when people come over, we want to impress. How would you feel if Jesus stopped by? We get so insecure about opening up our homes and our lives because we want everyone to see us at our best, some perfect version of us that doesn't exist. So we either go to crazy lengths to be perfect hosts or we just give up on hospitality all together. But when we try to project a perfect image, we aren't really letting people in so it's not really hospitality at all! You're showing them some other life that doesn't exist. It's not going to be perfect or convenient or play out the way you want it to. Be hospitable anyway!

Hospitality takes effort but you can do it. Speaking of inconveniences, without modern refrigeration, bread had to be made on the spot out of flour and yeast. Enough would be kneaded and baked every morning for the day but if you required more because of unexpected guests you had to make fresh bread! Same goes for meat. Without deep chest freezers you had to let your proteins walk around in the yard until it was time for dinner.

Abraham makes sure his guests feet get washed, bread gets made and a handpicked calf gets butchered. He's urgent and purposeful about making them feel taken care of. It's not about him. It's all about them.

When was the last time you showed hospitality for someone? You served them just to serve them? No agenda. That's important because we don't need to do hospitality as an evangelism trick. If we show true hospitality Jesus will shine through!

Maybe you are afraid that you'll be bad at hospitality. Truly anyone can do it. We're going to see in our training this week: Jesus was amazing at hospitality and he didn't even have a house! So there goes the "my house is too small or too messy or too whatever" excuse. Here's how you can do hospitality:

The complete and exhaustive guide to being hospitable:

1. Pray for the people you invite—ask God for ideas that will help you encourage them.
2. Give them food and a chance to talk.
3. That's seriously it! **Pray - Eat - Talk - Repeat**.

Food is essential. There is always food with worship and there should always be food in hospitality. Abraham knew this thousands of years ago. It's still true. Imagine going to a super bowl party that had no food...weird. What would the football watchers do during commercials? What would the commercial watchers do during football?

So feed your friends and future friends. No need to be elaborate, just a snack will do. You don't have to kill a calf but hamburgers might just hit the spot! Eat food and then make room for conversation.

The conversation is the best part of this story because Jesus wasn't having any of Sarah's lies. Isaac is eventually born and his name means "He laughs". Talk about a memorable night of hospitality!

Talking with people might not be your thing. You can do it over games, on a walk outside, or in a way that helps you to be more comfortable. In a world of tweets and status updates people are starving for conversation and we're all getting worse at it. This is another thing that hospitality is an antidote for!

See what God reveals through your hospitality

After eating and talking, Jesus decides to let Abraham in on the very plan of God and it leads to an amazing prayer for the lost people of Sodom and Gomorrah. When we show hospitality, since we are not in control of the outcome, we have to be ready to see what God might reveal.

We had a birthday party for my 6-year-old daughter recently and we invited her whole class. We didn't know who would come but 10 kids RSVP'd. One of the children had trouble earlier in the school year so my daughter Emelia and my wife Beth had been praying for her behavior. Beth would ask Emelia how this little girl was doing and we wondered how God would answer their prayers.

Well out of everyone that came, Beth had a great talk with that girl's mom and got to hear what was going on and get more insight into how God was working. Her behavior was getting better and afterward we were able to talk with Emelia about how she had prayed and how God heard her. So hospitality allowed us to minister to this mom but also to our own daughter!

This is hospitality week! What will God do with your hospitality? What will he reveal as you simply provide food and conversation for the people you've been praying for?

Maybe you don't have anything set up. It can be as simple as asking a co-worker to join you for lunch or having one neighbor over. It doesn't have to be a party or anything elaborate. Just prayer beforehand, food and conversation. You can do this!

And here's what God can do when we are hospitable:

Entertaining Angels

He can give angels their wings. Actually there's no definitive scripture that says angels have wings in the Bible and definitely nothing about it happening when a bell gets rung, but what I mean is God can make angels through our hospitality.

The word for angel in Greek is the same as the word for messenger. After all, that's what angels were, messengers from God. *Aggellos* is the word in Greek for both. So when we read Hebrews 13:1-2 and it says that people have been hospitable to *aggellos* unawares, it could be referring to angels or messengers. There's really no way to know.

Most major translations render it angels. I think they do this with Genesis 18 in mind (and it's just cooler). And it certainly could be that Christians had washed feet and made bread and had conversations with angels from heaven. More likely, however, is that Christians showed hospitality to strangers who came through their town by washing their feet, giving food and conversation and then through the course of conversation realized they were showing hospitality to a fellow Christian. Maybe one with a letter to a church or a message for Christians in some other city. How amazing would that conversation have gone? You're getting to know someone and they cautiously tell you they believe in Jesus, fearing you might be a persecutor who will turn them over to Rome. You wanted to tell them about your faith and had the same caution. But now you can both talk freely about your faith! I can imagine our ancient brothers and sisters staying up all night sharing stories about their churches and what God was doing in their lives.

In our local fellowship we have this dream to be a 1% church for the Lansing area. It's a big dream for us but a small thing for God. We believe that if just 1% of our area truly followed Christ it would change our whole area. The schools, our commutes, the hospitals—everything would be better. With present populations that would put us at over 4000 members in our church. Now, apply this lesson on hospitality to a church of 4000. You probably wouldn't know 3,800 of the members. So when you show kindness to a stranger or a new neighbor moves in or a new co-worker starts at your job, you may very well be entertaining a fellow messenger of the gospel! As God grows our church, I believe one day we'll all be entertaining angels in this way.

But we don't have to wait to be a big church. We can start now. This is how powerful hospitality is. *God uses it to* **make** *angels.* We've had so many people over who weren't Christians. We make food and talk and eventually do Bible studies and bring them to church. God works in their hearts until they make Jesus the Lord of their life and start spreading the message at their schools and workplaces. They have become messengers of God. If you're saved, this probably sounds like your story. Hospitality helped make you into a messenger of God!

We've had others over who believed and had been baptized but there wasn't much of a message coming from their lives because of sin or discouragement. Through hospitality—prayer, food and conversation—they were restored to be able to share about Jesus again. Through hospitality they got their wings back so they could be an angel again, a messenger of the good news.

I don't know where you are right now but I bet you could benefit from practicing hospitality. You may be in need of the hospitality that will allow you to hear the word of God and become a disciple of Jesus. What I love about our fellowship is that we make disciples through conversation and usually food. It's not some sterile class about the gospel. It's getting to know people and truly ministering to them. It's being messengers of the gospel. If that's where you are then pray for an opportunity to accept hospitality from a true Christ follower and watch as you are made into a messenger of the gospel by the power of the gospel.

Others may be in a place where we know God but we are down and don't have much of a message. You might need to take the bold step of asking if you can come and spend time with someone who can help you. Just show up at the front door—maybe with a phone call or a text first.

And the place where I hope you are is the place where you can invite others in for hospitality. Pray for them, feed them and talk—follow the Spirit—if you are connected with God it will become a God talk.

Hospitality Jump Start

Here are a couple of things you might be able to do right away with a little planning that will transform your hospitality and allow God to use you as his messenger.

1. Get in the habit of doing lunch with people after church. This could be members, this could be people you bring or new people that you meet that morning. This is a great way to do hospitality: lunch out or at your house.

2. Go through personal Bible studies to make Christians with more urgency. It should only take a few weeks to teach someone the Scriptures they need to understand to make Jesus Lord, fall in love with God, and fall in love with the church. A lot of times people would study more frequently but we have this habit of just doing one Bible study a week and miss out on the opportunity for more. Hospitable gospel messengers drop everything to help someone get Jesus in their life!

Hunting Down Hospitality

Read
Romans 12:9-13

Here Paul fires off a list of what the Christian life should be. If you're ever bored and wonder what to do as a Christian you can close your eyes and point to this paragraph. Obviously I want to focus on verse 13. We are to contribute to each other's needs and seek to show hospitality. Other versions say pursue hospitality—go after it, **hunt it down.**

Hospitality isn't just going to happen. You have to make a decision that you'll pray for someone or a group of people (neighbors, co-workers, gym buddies, coffee shop employees). Recently, I ordered pizza for the Starbucks employees where I write my lessons just to encourage them and to show them that I'm grateful for what they do even though it's their job. Who knows what the Spirit will do with that?

Make the decision to pray and then figure out the time and food and conversation for those people you're praying for. Let your walls and boundaries be broken. Allow people not just into your home but into your life. This week you'll see the master at work in six hospitality encounters with Jesus.

We take communion every week. Food and conversation and prayer. Every single week Jesus invites us to eat and drink with him, to pray and to talk in communion. He's letting us in. Jesus is alive and with us and still showing us hospitality to this day through the practice of communion. How amazing!

Let your weekly communion lead you to let others into your life by practicing the fine art of hospitality just like Jesus.

Week 6: In the Field Training

Peek at the Week

This week is all about hospitality. Hospitality is more than just hosting or entertaining. It's **Letting People In** to our lives, not just our homes. We'll see this in the ministry of Jesus this week. **Practice hospitality this week!** It's about being authentic, not perfect—anyone can do it! You can have people over for food and conversation, you can meet at a diner or coffee shop, you can host a game night or a bonfire. The most important thing is to provide an opportunity for the Spirit to turn strangers (in the church or outside of the church) into friends and true brothers and sisters in Christ.

Family Activity

Take a group picture or selfie of your hospitality night and tag it **#Hometown-Missionary #LettingPeopleIn** on social media. Put a **Mission Memo** on your **Mission Map** where you had your hospitality night. Monday's activity can be completed below:

Hospitality Hangups

1. _____

2. _____

3. _____

4. _____

Looking Ahead: Bible TALKS!

Even as we enjoy our Hospitality Nights, we are looking ahead to a more focused kind of hospitality: The Bible Talk. In two weeks, we'll learn about Bible talks and how God can use his word to transform our hometowns. To be successful, you need to start planning now, even before you learn what having a Bible talk is all about. Relax, you got this! Start by simply filling out the form below and beginning to spread the word. There are four Bible talk starters in Appendix on page 237, if you need help with your topic.

I will host a Bible Talk at _____ on _____

I will invite _____

Christians joining me _____

Topic _____

*Get the kids involved by making invitations together and passing them out at your hospitality night!

Monday: Come and See _____

Read
John 1:35-51

Examine
How can you be hospitable when you don't even have a house? Jesus is merely staying somewhere. Yet he is quick to let people in. We may think letting people in means opening our front door to a perfect home but truly inviting others "in" doesn't even require a home! Moreover, you could have people in your house every day of the week and never actually invite people into your life.

Perhaps, the number one thing that keeps people from the life changing habit of hospitality is insecurity about what people will see in our homes. Messy rooms, messy kids, a messy marriage, and, if you are following Jesus, a living savior redeeming all of those messes (Except maybe the rooms!). I don't know exactly what the place where Jesus was staying was like but I can guarantee the floors were dirtier than yours since they were probably made of dirt!

What if you just let people in? Tidy up but don't scour the house. Let it look like it usually looks. Don't have that talk with your kids about being polite. Let them be themselves. If you're entertaining Christians, they might get to see how your family really runs and offer loving advice. If you're reaching out to people who need Christ, being genuine will go a lot farther than shiny floors.

It can't be overstated: Jesus had no place to lay his head and converted four of his followers by simply saying "come and see" my life. "Let's spend the afternoon together." I love food and make a heavenly triple layer nacho—but my nachos aren't actually getting anyone to heaven. It's the time spent with people, not the perfect house, food or family.

If Jesus can help four people find him, who would go on to change the whole world, and he didn't even have a house, we have to throw out all of our excuses that keep us from practicing hospitality.

Apply

What keeps you from hospitality? What excuses keep you from letting people into your home? Your life?

Do

Write down your hospitality hang ups and then write how Jesus can redeem each of those things and use what you see as weaknesses to impact the people that you let in.

Yield

Lord give me the strength to let people in...

Tuesday: Inviting Jesus to the Wedding _____

Read

John 2:1-12
Luke 14:12-24

Examine

There are two sides to the hospitality coin. There's the extension of hospitality. Some of us love this and some of us hate it. Regardless, it's essential that we learn to be hospitable. The other side of the coin can be just as loathsome for some: receiving hospitality. Some people hate to be served, encouraged, fed, cared for, let in. Maybe it's a fear that you'll be expected to return hospitality. Maybe it's a pride/ insecurity thing. How do you respond when people invite you into their homes or lives? Is it an automatic 'no' when someone asks if they can help you? Being on the receiving end of hospitality can carry many of the same pressures as being a host. We want to be perfect guests (what does that even mean?). We don't want people to perceive us as being in need of help or encouragement. We don't want to portray weakness.

Jesus was the guest at a wedding. Before he had done anything miraculous or really kicked his ministry into gear; his "hour has not yet come," he's at a wedding reception in Cana. He's enjoying food and drink and dancing. It's often said, "You invited Jesus to the wedding, now keep him in the marriage." Ouch! But can you imagine if Jesus really was at your wedding? My preconceived image of Jesus tells me he'd be stiff and rigid and the opposite of the life of the party. But I bet the exact opposite is true. He's so into the party that even though his time hasn't come and he hasn't done any miracles, he agrees to turn water into wine so the people can drink more. (There are some really cool theological implications with this beyond drinking wine that I wish I could get into!)

Here's the takeaway regarding hospitality: When we accept hospitality; I mean go all in when we're invited to lunch or a righteous party or a game night, *the miraculous can break out!* Willingly accepting hospitality stretches us into God miracle territory. It may seem strange that eating people's food and hanging out in their homes would matter at all and yet it's in just such an environment that Jesus performs his very first miracle. Moreover, Jesus describes the kingdom as a wedding banquet. We were all once poor and blind strangers to God but our salvation rests in accepting his hospitality. Saying yes to being a guest readies us for the banquet in God that will never end.

Apply

What kind of miracles might happen when you willingly and joyfully accept hospitality? Are you a begrudging guest or a giving guest? We falsely think that providing for people builds trust but accepting hospitality and favors from others (allowing people to serve you, letting them in) actually builds more trust than serving them. Maybe this is because it actually takes more vulnerability to say yes and be a guest!

Do

Accept the next invitation you receive from a church member, friend, co-worker or fellow student. Go with joy and watch for miracles!

Yield

Lord, help me to bring true life to the parties and events I'm invited to...

Wednesday: Breaking Through Boundaries ____

Read
Mark 1:29-34

Examine

Another great but scary aspect of hospitality is that when we welcome people into our homes and lives, we are giving up some control. We can't know exactly what our guests will do, how long they'll stay, or what they need. Overcoming this challenge and bringing people into our homes anyway puts us in miracle territory. God can do amazing things when we allow hospitality to break through our boundaries.

Again, Jesus doesn't have a home of his own but he's staying with Peter in Capernaum. Peter's mother-in-law is ill and Jesus heals her. She immediately gets up and starts serving Jesus and the disciples. Jesus enables her to show hospitality by healing her.

Here's another benefit of being an imperfect host when we entertain Christians. Dinner isn't ready, there's laundry that needs folded, there's clean up that needs to be done after. What a great opportunity for fellowship and hospitality that goes both ways! If we're going to be radically hospitable and pursue it, then we're going to need help. Consider hosting non-Christian and Christian friends together. Your spiritual family can serve those whom you want to impact for Christ!

Here's what happens when Jesus miraculously enables Peter's mother-in-law to serve: Jesus stayed up late into the night healing an entire town. How would we respond if someone knocked on our door late in the evening? Are we willing to venture out to help those who are struggling when it's really late or really early? Would people even call us late in the night or have we defined our boundaries so well that people wouldn't want to bother us? Do we want to live an unbothered life? Or do we want to be used to heal our cities?

Apply

Think about how people perceive you. Are you the kind of person who can't be bothered? If so, think about what God things and Spirit adventures you might be missing out on.

Do

Before your next hospitality time pray about removing boundaries and norms that might be holding God back from the miraculous. When you do host, think about ways that you could get help from your Christian guests.

Yield

Lord, work miracles through my hospitality...

Thursday: Breaking Through the Boundaries of the Religious and the Non-Religious _____

Read
Luke 7:36-50
Luke 19:1-10

Examine

How do we reach the religious? How can we show Jesus to people who already think they know Jesus but are actually just following rules, ideas or traditions about Jesus? We often end up debating scriptures and failing to land on common ground. If you think about it, using religion to reach the religious doesn't really make much sense.

Hospitality may just be the thing that can break through. Show them Jesus by letting them into your Christ filled life and then you may be able to tell them about Jesus and the gospel. Jesus was the guest of religious people like the Pharisees. Their sensibilities were challenged by Jesus' guests and his words. This dinner party turns into an amazing and challenging display of God's grace. The woman receives mercy and religious Simon gets his world turned upside down by Jesus' words.

In the same way, our non-religious friends probably shudder at the thought of going to church or reading the Bible with us but who doesn't want to eat nachos and enjoy sweet hospitality? What I love about Jesus' conversation with Zacchaeus is that he is urgent. He sees that Zack has opened up to him and doesn't suggest getting together in a week or two. He says, "I must stay at your house today." Are we willing to drop what we have going on in order to show someone the love of Jesus?

We look at belief, repentance and baptism as a saving response to the gospel. But we could easily add talks over coffee, game nights with no agenda besides sharing love, and times of hospitality as salvation moments if we look back and consider what brought us to Christ and what will truly help our neighbors.

Apply

Look at the names on your prayer banner. How could you serve the religious and non-religious people on your list? How could hospitality with no agenda besides seeing what the Spirit does make an eternal difference for these people?

Do

Set up some intentional times of hospitality with the religious and non-religious people in your life. Pray for wisdom and have fun! **The next time you have a friend at church make sure you go to lunch with them that day after church.**

Yield
Lord, use my hospitality to reach the lost in my life...

Friday: Radical Non-Judgment

Read
John 8:1-11
John 12:47-50

Examine
Today's reading is about our hearts when we practice hospitality. Hospitality is letting strangers in. This includes people that we "know" but don't really know. This is the first step in transforming the strangers in our lives into friends and in God's timing, brothers and sisters in Christ. In this passage, a stranger is caught in sin and brought before Jesus. How will he treat her? How will he treat her accusers? This conversation was scandalous 2000 years ago and remains shocking to readers to this day.

Even if we believe that there is no judge besides God and that we should not judge (as the scriptures clearly teach), we must take a step back and let this sink in: even the one who can judge decides not to judge. Of course the stone throwers drop their stones and walk away. But Jesus was one without sin. Why does he not judge? He will return and there will be judgment but this is not the time for judgment. This is the time for encouragement, acceptance of weakness and opportunities to repent.

Can you be hospitable without being judgmental? Sounds easy enough but hospitality (letting people in and learning about who they really are and what they really struggle with) can be a breeding ground for judgment. And judgment kills hospitality—no matter how good the nachos are! When we let strangers in it is crucial that we are radically non-judgmental. Judgment is God's job. Do we think we can do a better job than God?

Can you practice radical non-judgment? What about when you find out that people are making bad life choices? What about when you hear that they struggle with pornography or same-sex attraction? What about if they have different political views? What if they have a criminal past or are participating in illegal behaviors even now? What if they are Muslim or atheist? Do any of those questions set you off? Can you fully love each of those people? We need to judge our judgmental hearts! We often rationalize our judgment by saying we don't want to become soft on sin. Being radically non-judgmental is NOT being soft on sin. It is admitting, like all the men holding stones before Jesus, that we all have sin and that judgment is not helpful. Love is helpful. Hospitality opens the door for the gospel that can save. Judgment only causes people to hide their sin. Non-judgmental, loving, encouraging help brings sin into the open so it can be dealt with by Jesus—the one who judges and saves. Jesus himself (again, the only one who could judge) believed and practiced radical non-judgment. Will you?

Apply
How have you been judgmental? How have you rationalized your attitudes? Can you think of a way to not compromise your beliefs and still let people in so they can experience the love of Christ before he comes for judgment?

Do
Do not judge! Just don't! Leave it to God and figure out how God can use you to help people open themselves up to the gospel (let the gospel in).

Yield
Father, I'm done with judging other people, use me to reach all kinds of people through love...

Saturday: The Great Banquet

Read
Revelation 4:1
Revelation 21:1-6
Revelation 22:1-5

Examine
Maybe you've never seen it like this before, but the entire story of the Bible could be seen as God's desire to be hospitable to us. He wants to let us in. This was the experience of Eden where God gave the first people everything they needed and walked with them. Sin entered and separation occurred but God never gave up.

When we make Jesus Lord, God lets us in. He shows us heavenly hospitality by providing for our needs and walking with us. But it's nothing like the hospitality we'll experience when heaven comes down and Jesus comes back. It will be like the garden has returned within the city of God, the New Jerusalem. God himself will be there and he'll intimately care for us, wiping away our tears with his own hand. This is our hope in Christ! This is the heavenly hospitality that we are waiting for!

When we practice hospitality like we've seen this week we are doing more than hosting a dinner or buying coffee. We are bringing glimpses of the restoration to come into our broken world. We are answering Jesus' prayer that God's "will be done on earth as it is in heaven". Do you want to see heaven? Do you want to speed his coming and bring as many with you as possible into eternity? Be hospitable. Provide opportunities for the Spirit to make strangers into friendships that will last forever.

Who knew hospitality was so powerful?! When Christians let people in and lovingly provide for the needs of others we are painting a picture of heaven for a world that has lost sight of the glorious eternity to come.

Apply

What's the most heavenly hospitality experience you've had as a Christian? What made it so good? Why do you think the simple act of letting people in is so powerful?

Do

Host a time of hospitality. Don't skip this week's activity. When you sow hospitality, you will yield heavenly results.

Yield

Lord use my time of hospitality to bring a glimpse of the glory to come into my world...

Week 7: Heroes of the Faith—
New Testament

Concerning this salvation, the prophets who prophesied about the grace that was to be yours searched and inquired carefully, inquiring what person or time the Spirit of Christ in them was indicating when he predicted the sufferings of Christ and the subsequent glories. It was revealed to them that they were serving not themselves but you, in the things that have now been announced to you through those who preached the good news to you by the Holy Spirit sent from heaven, things into which angels long to look.

—1 Peter 1:10-12

What's the good life?

We've all got a picture of it in our minds, in our hearts. The ideal.

You at your best. Your family thriving. Imagine it now—the wealth you want, spouse and kids, a healthy reflection in the mirror, meaningful work and fun hobbies. It's easy, like the best day of vacation stretched out over years...the good life. Close your eyes and think about it for a moment. Can you see it?

The quest for the ideal life fills the shelves of bookstores in the form of diet and self-help books. There's even a place where you can temporarily experience the good life with your family appropriately named "The Magic Kingdom". It's magic because when you go there you are the center of attention and everything is catered to your happiness. I think we all have a magic kingdom—an ideal picture of life. Keep your picture in mind as you read.

1 Peter 1:10-12

The prophets and patriarchs of the Old Testament were desperately searching for the kingdom of God. The angels were on the edge of their seats wondering how and when the kingdom of God would come to the earth. They talked about it and dreamt about it. Maybe they wondered how God might do it. They had their redemption theories. Maybe God will do this. Maybe it will happen at this time or that. They longed for a glimpse of salvation. I'd love to hear those angelic conversations and listen in on their speculation. It would be amazing to hear their reactions as they actually saw God's redemptive plan play out with Judas' betrayal and Jesus' suffering and resurrection.

This is so amazing: We know how God did it! His Son's willing sacrifice and demonstration of power over death and sin won our salvation on the cross and in the empty tomb. The Spirit initiated the kingdom of God at Pentecost. We know what the prophets could only dream about. We see what the angels longed to see. We live in God's saving grace as citizens of the kingdom. Do you understand how amazing it is to be saved and to live this life in the kingdom of God?

> *We need to be reminded sometimes because even though we've been given the kingdom of God, we often chase after competing kingdoms, those magic kingdoms that look good. We think they'll make us happy. We forget what God has given us.*

Go back to your idea of the good life. When you closed your eyes and pictured the good life did you see the kingdom of God? Do you believe that a God life is the real good life? Or have you begun chasing after a false kingdom?

There are a lot of authors and people that promise the good life, the best life if you just follow these steps, or invest here, or eat this miracle food. I've never made such a promise as a preacher or an author but I'm going to do it now: In Christ, as a soul living in the New Testament era, you can have the good life that the angels and prophets longed for.

Take a moment and imaginatively read Acts 2:42-47.

That's the good life.

I get duped sometimes by Satan, "the ruler of the kingdoms of the air," those magic kingdoms that never have and never will exist, into thinking that some other kingdom is the good life. More wealth, less illness, soreness, pain. Less sacrifice and more leisure. Less being bothered and more doing whatever I want. More pleasure. I think that's the good life sometimes. That's the kingdom I long for.

Do you remember what Jesus came proclaiming in Mark 1:15 *"The Kingdom of*

God is in your midst, repent and believe the gospel!" Jesus has revealed to us God's kingdom, God's ideal, the only good life. And he came saying "repent", change your ideas about the good life and believe the good news.

Jesus has made the good life, his kingdom, available to us. Are you living a kingdom life or are you longing for some other kingdom?

When we close our eyes and imagine the good life, this is what we should see:

Devotion—all in. I want my dreams and visions to be about how I gave my all to God and the church and how he used me to do his will and glorify his name. I want my picture of the good life to have a Bible open every day and notes scribbled or typed as the Holy Spirit leads me to new understanding about God. I want long walks spent in prayer getting to know God and becoming known by him. I want awe and wonders and signs that can only be attributed to God working in my life and the church. I want to close my eyes and dream of giving to those in need instead of piling up stuff for myself. I see visions of dinners with friends and singing around bonfires and talking about what Jesus has done over coffee. I want to value sacrifice and enjoy giving even when I'm tired or want to be alone. I want the kingdom every day in my life.

It strengthens my faith when I think about this kingdom vision because when the church is at its best, this is exactly what I see. God's vision for the kingdom is real and alive. I've seen Acts 2:42-47 lived out.

Will you dream about the good life in the kingdom with me?

Will you fight against the good looking imposters that trick us into thinking the easy life is the good life?

Are you feeling challenged and inspired? This walk is challenging but my hope is that you are inspired to live the God life that he has to offer you.

We have this word—it's actually falling out of favor—called conversion. When someone becomes a Christian, they are a convert. Conversion implies a wholesale change has happened. It means that they were one way and now they are another. Isn't that exactly what Jesus called us to do—to accept his vision of the kingdom and the good life? To convert our desires to his? So we aren't just winning souls and checking the salvation box for people. We are helping them convert to the kingdom life, the God life. This is why we do Bible studies that highlight discipleship and the church.

> *Are you ready for a radical thought: when you live the kingdom life, you will make disciples. You will convert souls for Christ by his power. It's just going to happen.*

How does Acts 2:42-47 end? After describing the life of a New Testament Christian what does it say was happening? The Lord added to their number day by day those who were being saved! When you immerse yourself in Christ's kingdom you will bear fruit, you will have an impact. It's just what happens.

But the opposite is also true. You could share your faith every day, do Bible studies, and never see someone converted to Christ if you aren't living in the kingdom that the angels longed to see. Helping people come to Christ is not merely saying a prayer or dunking them under water—it's helping them change allegiances, convert their desires, value the kingdom of God above their ideas of the good life. That can't happen if they aren't shown a tangible example of a New Testament Christian living the true good life of love and sacrifice and devotion and awe.

And when people do see the kingdom, they are drawn to it like the angels were. What are we showing our friends, family, neighbors, classmates? Most don't open their Bibles to read about the kingdom of God—the only glimpse they get is you. They should be wondering at us. Confused by our joy. Taken aback by our love and selfless service. They should see the kingdom of God. They should see the passion within us for our Lord and saviour Jesus Christ!

So you want to actually live the good life? Live the kingdom life.

Here's what our minds do sometimes: we think the New Testament was some special time where amazing miracles happened and we look back with wonder in the same way the Old Testament heroes looked ahead and wondered. But here's the reality: we live in the New Testament Era. There is no difference. We're waiting for Jesus to come back just like they were. We have the Holy Spirit just like they did. If there is a difference, it's that we have the written Word, so in some ways we have even more. Why do we read about our brothers and sisters and think we can't have the same impact they had?

There is only one reason why we can't have the same impact as them: we don't have the same vision of the kingdom driving our lives. We settled for a counterfeit kingdom with worldly promises. Instead of living the kingdom life.

Read the passage below and you'll get a glimpse of what God can do when we dream about his kingdom and live the kingdom life.

Mark 4:3-8

The word: the prophets, the gospels and the New Testament are a seed that falls on the soil of our hearts. We tend to think of this passage as 3 bad hearts before you become a Christian and the good heart of a Christian. But whenever the word is read or preached or pondered, it falls on our hearts as Christians in one of these ways. I'm sure there are times when Satan is attacking and the word doesn't even get a foothold. There are times when we hear a message and forget it because it doesn't sink in. And quite frequently I believe that the word gets choked out by the thorny competing visions of the kingdom. I don't want to focus on those first 3 soils though. Look at the kingdom heart, the good soil, that receives and believes in Christ's vision of the good life, the person who acts like Acts 2:42-47.

Jesus explains this 4th soil later in verse 20 saying, *"Those who are sown on the good soil are the ones who hear the word of God and accept it and bear fruit, thirtyfold and sixtyfold and a hundredfold."*

If you reject the "good life" and live the God life in his kingdom it's not a question of if you will be fruitful or if you'll help convert someone by God's power. The question is 30, 60 or 100? How much impact will you have?

In our church we used to look at this scripture when the church was much smaller, when our membership was stuck in the 30s for years, and wonder what it would look like if our church grew. And then it started growing! Up into the 60s in just a couple of years and now into the 100's. 30, 60, 100. It's not just a cool thing that happened in the New Testament. It's what God is doing now with his New Testament people who live today.

What will it be for you—30, 60 or 100? When you meet God how many people will be there with you because of God's work in your life? How many people will you impact—30, 60, 100?

One last note to remember: You won't have 30 fold or 100 fold impact by focusing on having an impact. You have that kind of impact by making the soil right. Making your heart right. Getting that kingdom focus and watching as God makes things grow.

God makes it grow. We're still a part of the Kingdom that Peter preached into existence in Acts 2 and it'll keep on growing as long as it's filled with kingdom people and New Testament heroes like you.

Week 7: In the Field Training

Peek at the Week

This week we'll avoid the more common New Testament heroes like Peter and Paul and learn from the lesser known disciples who made it onto the pages of scripture through their devotion to God and openness to the Spirit. The writing of the New Testament finished with John's "Amen" at the end of Revelation but the Spirit of the New Testament lives on in all disciples of Christ. As you read about some behind the scenes heroes, imagine what could be written about you as you share your faith and follow the Spirit's lead.

Like the Old Testament heroes from week 5, the goal is not to just read and be inspired but to imitate and be an inspiration yourself. These 6 challenges should be the activities we dream of as disciples. They'll surely take more than a week to accomplish but through living a kingdom life and praying to be a spiritual hero, God can write a story with your life that will impact 30, 60 or even 100 fold. If you want to share insights from this week's lesson or devotionals use **#HometownMissionary #3060or100** on social media.

Activity

Be A New Testament Hero: Pray Through These Challenges of a Lifetime
- Be on God's side of the Spirit's saving work in someone's life.
- Intentionally encourage someone so much that it changes their life.
- Devote yourself to a place and the people in it until God produces fruit.
- Have someone in your home and teach them the Bible.
- Raise the standard for raising your children beyond them becoming Christians to becoming Christians with spiritual vision (more on what this means in Friday's devotional).
- Walk with someone from the deserts of life to the waters of baptism and beyond.

When you read this list, who comes to mind? Who could you reach out to in these ways? This week's training will examine the New Testament Heroes behind each of these challenges and inspire you to dream big for the kingdom today.

Have a Family Devotional Dream Session

Gather together and ask everyone to draw a picture of the good life and then discuss what they drew. Teach your family about God's good kingdom life and pray together about the God life.

*Don't forget to talk and pray about next week's Bible talk!

Monday: Ananias—You can be on God's side of the Spirit's saving work in someone's life _____

Read
Acts 9:1-19

Examine

True visions from the Spirit come in pairs. In Acts 10, Peter has a vision that compliments Cornelius' vision and allows his whole family and all non-Jewish people to be welcomed into the Kingdom. In this chapter we meet Paul, who will play a huge role in the gentile mission and we can thank Ananias' boldness and surrender for that.

Saul/Paul receives his vision as Jesus himself rebukes him and temporarily blinds him. Paul thought he knew God and saw God's vision for his life but when he finally hears the voice of the true God he says, "Who are you, Lord?" He didn't know God at all and the blindness that follows highlights the true state of his heart. You'd think that a conversation with Jesus himself would be enough to save a person but there's another side to this vision. As Saul is being blinded on the road to Damascus, Ananias is being blindsided by a request from Jesus: Find Saul of Tarsus, the infamous Christian persecutor, the last person you'd want to run into if you were a Christian, and heal his blindness. I love the Bible's honesty. Ananias doesn't leap at the opportunity to reach out to a murderer. He talks back to Jesus! But he gets his heart right and sets out to meet Saul. The scales fall off and Ananias is the first face Saul sees with his regained sight and reborn faith. We learn in Acts 22:16 that Ananias knew exactly what to say next, *"And now why do you wait? Rise and be baptized and wash away your sins, calling on his name."*

We are introduced to Ananias in Acts 9:10 in the most simple way: *"There was a disciple at Damascus…"* Acts 22 tells us more, *"He was a devout man…"* And that's all we know. What does God look for in a person that he wants to use to be on the other side of a miracle? Well he just needs a devout disciple. How many conversion stories will be written of you that begin, "There was a disciple in your town, at your work, at your school…" A devoted disciple is all God needs to change the world one soul at a time.

Apply

Have you heard the Spirit's voice recently to reach out to someone? How have you responded? Even Ananias struggled but eventually surrendered to God. Talk to God about what you are feeling like Ananias did and maybe you'll find yourself fulfilling your half of a miracle.

Do

Share your faith with that person God has been telling you to share with. Know and believe that just as you've been prompted by the Spirit, the Spirit has been working on them as well.

Yield

Lord, I will stop fighting the Spirit so I can be the other half of a miracle...

Tuesday: Barnabas—You can encourage someone so much that it changes their life _____

Read

Acts 4:32-37
Acts 13:1-4

Examine

We underestimate the power of encouragement. We may merely think of little encouragement cards (which are great!) but encouragement is so much more than a thoughtful note. The word means to give courage. And oh how we need courage as disciples of Jesus Christ. The opposite of encouragement is discouragement—how many of us feel discouraged and wish we could snap out of it? Encouragement is what we need!

Barnabas' nickname was Son of Encouragement. He was an encourager and a giver and God used that mindset to do amazing things through his life and to take him all over the world. Acts 13 is a milestone for Christianity. Paul, the apostle to the gentiles, is sent out from Antioch after a time of prayer and fasting. But upon further examination it's not just Paul and he's not even the first name listed. It's Barnabas, the encourager! The influence will shift after a while but the Spirit first sends Barnabas and Paul. Moreover, we might think they had some grand plan for saving the world but their first stop is Cyprus. Why Cyprus? That's where Barnabas is from. It's as if the Spirit sent them out and they didn't know where to go so Barnabas said, "Let's go to my mom's house." And that's how the world was evangelized!

Encouragement is powerful enough to be a driving force behind the spread of Christianity in the first century. We don't give encouragement, we unleash it. And then the Spirit does more than we could ever imagine. Encouragement rarely happens by accident. It doesn't take much but it does take forethought and prayer. Will you be a son or daughter of encouragement? Where will God take you and how will you impact the world when you decide to give encouragement?

Apply

There are many ways to bear fruit and have an impact. Maybe there is a lost person in your life who could be eternally impacted by your intentional acts of encouragement? Or, maybe there is a Christian in your ministry or church that has been discouraged. You can bear fruit through them by encouraging them so they can get back up and get out on the mission field.

Do

Thoroughly encourage someone. Pray and think about who needs it and how to do it and then watch where God takes it!

Yield

God, I want to be a son or daughter of encouragement...

Wednesday: Jesus in Galilee—Devote yourself to a place and people until God produces fruit _____

Read

Matthew 4:12-17

Examine

Okay, this is definitely not about one of the lesser knowns of the New Testament. This is about Jesus himself but it reveals a lesser known truth about how Jesus shared his faith. We are conditioned to imagine Jesus going from town to town and making disciples (which he did) but before that at the beginning of his ministry he lived in one dark place and lived as a light from inside of it.

Maybe you've heard of having a "fishing hole" where you can build relationships and share your faith as a "fisher of men." Jesus' fishing hole was a fishing town on the northern shore of the Sea of Galilee. It was in Capernaum that he called Peter, Andrew, James and John to leave their nets and old lives behind and follow him.

Preaching the gospel is less about shining a light on sin or having a laser beam focus on evangelism. It's about shining forth wherever you go. By living in Galilee, Jesus fulfilled the words of Isaiah that a light would dawn in a dark place. Galilee was nothing special but Jesus' presence made it special. With Christ living inside of us we can be a great light to all the places we go and turn the coffee shop, gym, office or classroom into fishing holes that God can use to make disciples who will make more disciples and change the whole world. He did it once and he can do it again in your life!

Apply
Where could your fishing hole be? You may not share your faith there all the time but you'll go with the mindset of shining the light of Christ and being open to the Spirit. Get to know the people there and love them like Jesus did in Galilee.

Do
Choose a place that will be your fishing hole. Every time you visit pray that the light of Christ could spark saving conversions.

Yield
Lord, this is my fishing hole...use me as a light there...

Thursday: Priscilla and Aquila—Have someone in your home and teach them the Bible _____

Read
Acts 18:1-4, 24-28
Romans 16:3-5

Examine
Priscilla and Aquila are often seen as the New Testament's power couple. The reality is a little less glamorous. They had the same skills as Paul, making tents. They probably lived in a style of home that had a workshop on the first floor and living space above (kind of like those cool downtown lofts above coffee shops). They let Paul work with them during the week and use their space since he refused monetary support from some churches he ministered to. On the weekends he would preach and Priscilla and Aquila opened their home to be used as a church. Maybe the large tent-making space downstairs was converted into a gathering space on Sunday or maybe they used the homey part upstairs. However we imagine it, the

impact of this full time working couple who used their resources and their home for the kingdom can't be overstated. Paul sees them as lifesavers and surely Apollos would say the same.

After Paul left Corinth, a devout believer named Apollos, who it seems had heard about Jesus but not heard the full gospel, came into town and preached powerfully but with some missing parts in his message. What's the solution? Did they need an evangelist or full-time minister to talk to Apollos? No. They just needed a Godly couple to open their home and teach the scriptures. Priscilla and Aquila knew just what to do. They studied the (OT) Bible with Apollos and he became a great asset to the early church. These aren't super apostles; just house church leaders with open doors, open hearts and an open Bible.

Apply

Who could you open your home to and study with? Maybe you lack the confidence to study the Bible with someone. The best way to learn is to do it. The word of God is the power of salvation. Stick your neck out and start having some saving conversations!

Do

Study the Bible with someone. You got this! (Well God does.)

Yield

Lord, open my heart so I may open my home to my friend...

Friday: Philip—Raise the standard for Child rearing beyond them becoming Christians _____

Read
Acts 21:7-9

Examine

We'll get more back story on Philip tomorrow. He was last seen on the desert road to Ethiopia and then preaching in various towns in Acts 8. Now, years later we learn that he has a house (and presumably a house church and a wife) in the seaside town of Caesarea Maritima. Luke, the author of Acts, is with Paul on his journey to Jerusalem as they stop in Caesarea and he is impressed by the spirituality of Philip's daughters. They are pure and they prophesy.

If you are a disciple of Jesus with children, then I'm sure you pray for your children. The common prayer is for our children to be disciples which is awesome. But what if we prayed more ambitious kingdom prayers for our kids and took more ambitious kingdom action? If you have a family, then you are more than just a hometown missionary, you are a home missionary.

Philip's daughters prophesied. That may be referring to the miraculous gift of the Holy Spirit but it could also be a more simple reference to the girls' ability to look about them and apply the scriptures to their world and their lives. That's prophecy! I have two daughters and I want them to prophesy. I want them to have a God outlook on the world. Our Kid's Church is amazing, but it's merely a supplement to my home ministry. Am I teaching my girls to see the world with a Christian worldview? Am I shaping their lives to not become mere church goers, but pure prophetesses?

I'm amazed at the lengths parents go to for athletics. I'm trying to avoid the trap of overcommitment while still finding ways give my girls opportunities to have fun and socialize—it's tough! What does it teach them when they are expected to do tons of extracurricular activities for academics or athletics but church and church in the home (devotionals, prayers, special family time, hospitality) is neglected? We can't call our kids to sacrifice for a sports team and not call them to be radical about putting God first. That's not a mixed message—it's the wrong message!

Sometimes family time is used as an excuse to not do the mission (i.e. "I can't make time for the lost because I'm focusing on saving my family). This just doesn't hold up. Some of the proudest memories I have of my dad were some most embarrassing moments at the time. I remember at a street fair he shared with a whole group of (drunk) people outside of a party store. I remember him learning Spanish so he could street preach on his delivery route in Southwest Detroit. I remember so many people coming over for Bible studies or marriage counseling with my parents. I remember the people who didn't have cars that we would pick up on Sunday morning on the way to church. Yes, our kids are our greatest ministry but the best way to minister to them is to be active as a hometown missionary yourself! Our kids don't want to hear stories of the glory days. They want to see parents on fire for God. They only know your walk with God from what they can see right now.

Apply

What are your prayers for your kids? Are you asking God to make them great in his sight? What are your children seeing in your example as you follow Christ?

Do

Intentionally parent in a way that creates prophets. Prophets see the world through the lens of God's word. Do what you need to do to give your children spiritual vision.

Yield

Lord, make my family a ministry that glorifies you...

Saturday: Philip—Walk with somebody from the deserts of life to the waters of baptism and beyond

Read
Acts 8:26-40

Examine

Here we see young Philip being whisked here and there by the Spirit in the days before he "settled down" in Caesarea and led a house church. His encounter with the Eunuch is legendary, but it's also the experience of so many who make disciples or become disciples.

First, the Spirit moves. We're told how He moves in Philip through an angelic messenger. And we can assume the Eunuch is also moved after his trip to Jerusalem. It seems like was expecting some grand epiphany on his pilgrimage but he left his time of worship with more questions than answers. He's searching the scriptures but not able to figure out what Isaiah is talking about. So many of the people that the Spirit is leading us to are in a similar spot. They've had religious experiences that left them wanting but they have no one to help them see God through the haze of religion and/or secularism. That's where we can come in just like Philip.

We can walk with them and listen to them. We can hear their ideas about God and scripture and through prayer and the Spirit direct them out of the dry desert of confusion and into the life-giving waters of baptism. How can this happen? Well, all we need to do is listen for the Spirit and walk with the people that we're praying for. He'll make the opportunities clear when we pray.

Philip is so patient and sticks with the Eunuch, explaining the scriptures and showing him that Jesus is the suffering savior that Isaiah spoke of. The Old School Bible study series at the back of this book has this very passage in it! Your chariot ride with your friend may not be as quick and might have more bumps in the road but if you just stay with the people God has placed in your life, you'll surely get the opportunity to go down into the water (or stand next to a trough) and baptize them!

Apply

Who are you walking with? Do you see how the Spirit is working to make them open to the saving gospel? What could you do this week to move your friend out from the desert and closer to living water?

Do

This is a big one: **Study the Bible with someone**, helping them to fall in love with God and the church. Baptize them. God is on the move—go with him.

Yield

Lord, I want to walk with those you've put in my life, down into the waters of baptism and beyond, even to eternity...

Week 8: The Word of Life

In the beginning, God created the heavens and the earth. The earth was without form and void, and darkness was over the face of the deep. And the Spirit of God was hovering over the face of the waters. And God said, "Let there be light," and there was light.

—Genesis 1:1-3

Let me tell you about the power of the word of God:

I love reading about and dreaming about creation. The latest scientific ideas about our world intrigue me. I wonder as I walk through the woods and I think about my life, how did this happen? How is it that all of this exists and that I have life in me? No one has the answers to those questions but here's something we know from the very first sentences of scripture:

> God has spoken everything into existence. Everything that's here is here because of the power of his word.

I know most of us have probably read the creation account in Genesis 1 more than any other passage in the Bible as we set out to read the whole Bible only to run into Leviticus or Numbers and get stuck. But don't gloss over verse 3. God said, "Let there be light." And light began to exist and it's still shining! And God said let there be sky, water and land and creatures to fill the sky, water and land and let there be people, and here we are! The Bible doesn't get into the details of how God did this. The only thing that seems to be important is that all of this happened because God spoke it. He created a universe with a word, with a breath from his mouth. That's the power of the word of God.

Read Psalm 19:1-6

Theologians refer to the beginning of this passage as "General Revelation". General in that anyone anywhere can see a sunset and think about God. For me, a waterfall or a bird or looking at my children gives me this sense that there's something more to all of this. God's creation still speaks to us doesn't it?

But then the Psalm goes on to describe what theologians call "Special Revelation". This means that God has given us something special to reveal himself to us in an even greater way than creation.

Now read the rest: Psalm 19:7-11

That special revelation is his word. While the sun moving through the sky inspires awe: the law of the Lord is perfect—reviving the soul. The testimony sure, the precepts right—causing joy. The commandments and the rules—better than gold and sweeter than honey.

So yes, you can take a walk in the woods or sit by the water and be inspired by God, but God decided that wouldn't be enough so God wrote us a book. He put his word, powerful enough to create light and mountains and people, into writing so we could listen to it, so we could read it for ourselves anytime. You're holding the same word that has the power to create a universe in your hands when you open your Bible.

Why did God give us his word? Have you ever thought about that? He didn't have to, but this was his plan. He decided to let us in on the plan and even make us promises, to give us his word and make good on it.

I think there's another question that helps answer the question of why God gave us his word. Have you ever thought about why we can't see God? Wouldn't that make it a lot easier to follow him! But we can't see him. Why not? I think it's because seeing the entity that can create our universe would literally blow our minds. God tells Moses no one can see my face and live (Exodus 33:20) and he shows Moses his glory by showing him his back or his wake and by proclaiming his name to him as he was hidden in a cleft in the rock. No we can't see God, we can't handle it. We cry during commercials. We don't get to see God until he comes back at the end of all things when he makes everything new.

But God doesn't want to be hidden, so he reveals himself to us. Generally, through the glory of his creation that he spoke into existence, and specially by writing us a book so we could know him. Isn't that amazing that God would write a love letter to us so we could seek and find him in this life? How powerful is this book that God has blessed us with so we could see him come to life from these pages as we read since we can't actually look upon the creator and live! We are so blessed! What could be better than a personal love letter from God written over centuries?

Well there is one thing, check this out:

Read John 1:1-5, 14

So, every bit of creation cries out that there is a loving God. Amazing! And we have a love letter written by God himself so we could spend time listening to him and be transformed. Even more amazing! But for God that just wasn't enough. He wanted to be even more personal, so the word became flesh.

It's important to note that this wasn't Plan B. He decided at the beginning of everything, before he even said "Let there be light" that he'd give us himself. The word of God, logos in Greek means the plan or design. Jesus is God's plan in the flesh!

The Bible's description of God just gets more and more intimate, from creation to revelation to incarnation. In Jesus, God revealed himself to us personally. He lived this life as a part of creation. He interacted with and fulfilled the written word. The word of God lived and breathed and walked among us. And at the end of the Bible we're told that God will come and be with us in a new heaven and a new earth. We'll all get to see him and hear his voice and be with him. God's word, God's plan, fulfilled in the life of Jesus is so amazing and powerful and as personal as possible!

Now I hope that helps you if you've been struggling with having devotional times. We get to carry God's amazing word with us and read about the word made flesh! The Holy Spirit that orchestrated the scriptures also lives in us. We are so blessed! But the purpose of this chapter is not to give your devotional times a boost.

> *I have a question for you that I really want you to think about: what do you think is going to happen when you share the word of God with someone?*

If you've been reading this book for the last 8 weeks, you've probably thought about this a lot. It might make you quite anxious. I know what we think because I think it too:

—we think people say we're weird (even though people may already think that)

—we think we won't do it right

—we think we won't know what to say

—we think we'll lose a friend or it will make things awkward

What if instead of thinking those anxious thoughts, we thought about how powerful and personal and perfect God's word is? What if we thought, "I am sharing the words that can create a universe and reveal heavenly promises and be so personal that it's really alive?" I looked for verses that tell us to be afraid, or to be very afraid before we share the word of God but this is all I found. Go ahead and check them out:

Psalm 33:6
Psalm 107:19-20
Psalm 147:15
Isaiah 55:10-11
1 Corinthians 1:18

These passages tell us that when we open our Bibles and share God's word we are unleashing the power of creation, the power to heal, the urgency of God, the will of God that cannot be broken and the power of salvation. What if we thought about that instead of focusing on our fears and doubts? All of that happens, because of God, when we open our mouths and our Bibles at the same time. Now that's amazing!

But, what happens when we don't share the word of God?

Well check out **Romans 10:14-17.**

Paul is specifically talking to Israel, to people who had the written word of God but still needed to hear about Jesus Christ. We live in a similar society where we have more Bibles published than any book every year and yet people need to hear about Jesus Christ from us or they will not gain faith. They will not find salvation. There's only one thing that can stop God's saving word of life from being unleashed and doing its work—us! Are we who believe in the word muzzling the word? Is the world lacking faith because those with faith aren't sharing?

This is why Bible Talks (small group Bible discussions) are so amazing. The Bible talks. And when the Bible talks faith happens, God moves, power is unleashed. All you have to do is be there and open the word and watch what God can do!

Open the Bible with someone this week—truly share your faith!

Check out Acts 6:7, 19:20

When I think about the book of Acts, I think about the Spirit using Peter to start the church and Paul's missionary journeys and how the church grew and spread so much in such a short time. But it wasn't any of these men or even the greatness of the church that caused the increase that changed the whole world. It was the word!

When the word increases the church multiplies. That's Bible math! God's word, if and when we share it, will prevail. So have a gathering, a Bible talk in your home or at a local coffee shop or even at work during lunch. God's word is going to be opened and shared. It's going to get into people's hearts. It's going to fulfill God's purpose and make a difference. That's just what it does! Find someone to study the Bible with. Go for it this week. You'll look back on this week with eyes open wide and hair blown back a little as you witness the power of the word of life unleashed!

Week 8: In the Field Training

Peek at the Week

This week is all about sharing the Word of God. When the Bible talks, God's creativity, promises, intimacy and salvation are all unleashed! You should have your Bible talk set up. A Bible talk is simply a time of hospitality focused on sharing scripture and calling people to decisions. There are 4 starter Bible talk templates from the parable of Jesus in Appendix B on page 237, at the back of this book.

If you aren't hosting or attending a Bible talk, you could set up a Bible study with someone or you could simply share a scripture. When you host or attend a Bible Talk make sure to mark it on your mission map.

Challenge

This week's **one challenge is to share the word of life with someone** who needs to hear it. If you want to share your sharing experience, you can use **#hometownmissionary #Bibletalks.**

Upcoming: Gospel Night (Soul Talk)

Even as you prepare for your Bible talks, it's time to think about our next hometown missionary event. This one is bigger than your small group. If your church is doing this book together, then this event and invitations should be shared soon. If you're doing this on your own, talk to some leaders in your church and see if you can organize a Gospel Night. This night of teaching focused on the people we want to reach with the gospel. There is a discussion template in appendix C that focuses on one simple but deep question: "How's your soul?" This life and death discussion could be the spark that God will use to change our friends' eternity. When will you hold your gospel night and who will you invite?

I'm inviting and praying for these 3 people:

1_____

2_____

3_____

This week's reading might just be the spark you need to invite someone to hear the word of life at a Bible Talk, Bible Study, church or an upcoming Gospel Night!

For an easy family night devotional

- Sing!
- Read parts of Genesis 1 and John 1 (age appropriate) and talk about how God created us with his word
- Spend time praying for your Bible talks

Monday: Living and Active

Read

Hebrews 4:1-13

Examine

The last two verses of this passage may be some of the most familiar scriptures to us about the word of God. Sometimes familiarity can keep us from seeing the true power of a verse in its context. Even though we often share this passage with non-believers, like the rest of Hebrews, it is written as a warning to the faithful. In context, the Hebrew writer is urging Hebraic Christians to keep from hardening their hearts to the word of God and missing out on his rest (eternity). We can't think we're immune to losing our faith and missing out on God because we already have this example of Israel falling in the desert. God was willing to let an entire generation die because they stopped listening to his word!

When we get to verse 12 and hear that *"the word of God is living and active"* we should consider if this truth is true in our lives. Is the word of God alive for you? The word became flesh in Jesus Christ (John 1). God has made the word come to life, but that doesn't guarantee that it won't become just another dead book of inspirational quotes or platitudes for us. What would it take for you to read the Bible in a way that made it come to life? Journaling? Good spiritual books? Videos explaining scripture? Coloring or drawing? We are blessed with so many Bible resources today that can aid in inspiring us. There is no excuse for having dead devotional times. Maybe we don't see dead devotional times as a big deal. This passage teaches that when we allow our hearts to harden to God's word we miss out in the biggest way possible. What will it take to bring your reading back to life?

The importance of this is even bigger than our personal salvation. The word is alive and active. But I've never seen the word active in someone who's having dead devotional times or no devotional times at all. We need to make the word come to life in our lives so we will be active in sharing it. People share about what they love and people share about what's working. How easy is it for us to share about a good movie or TV show? How effortlessly do we promote diets that work for us? When God's word is alive—when you love it and it's working in your life—you will share your faith! And the word of God will become alive and active in someone else's life!

Apply
What's one thing you could add to your reading times to bring more life to them? A reading plan, journaling, lectio divina, a spiritual book, a podcast...? What has worked in the past? What will keep you engaged after these hometown missionary devotionals are done?

Do
Share what you read today with someone. Sharing the word causes us to learn more and lets the Spirit work in a non-threatening way that could have an eternal impact.

Yield
Lord, make your word alive and active in my life...

Tuesday: From House to House _____

Read
Luke 10:1-9
Acts 2:46, 5:42
Acts 16:13-15, 40

Examine
Have you ever considered how church "worked" in the first century? Christians did not have buildings or meeting halls. Sunday wasn't even a day off. It was the first workday of the week. Yet, our faith grew from the backwoods of Galilee to the household of Caesar himself in just a few decades and now it spans the whole world. We are not commanded to "do church" in the same way as our ancient brothers and sisters but we shouldn't neglect the church life principles that we see in the scriptures even as we apply them to a very different culture.

The early church grew from house to house. We don't need to abandon large church meetings. We are blessed to be able to congregate. But we do need to realize that large church meetings are not actually the church! Picture a map of your area with one dot where your church meets. Now picture the same map with a dot for every household in the church. Which is going to be more effective at reaching people with the gospel?

Being a Christian who goes to church produces the first map with one dot. Making your household into a church produces map number two and instantly saturates your city with gospel hotspots. This is exactly how the first church grew. It was Jesus' plan to send out disciples to find worthy households. These weren't just first century Airbnb's. These would become house churches after the disciples and Jesus left town. After Jesus ascended, the disciples followed this plan everywhere they went setting up house churches. Lydia's house church is the first that we know of on the continent of Europe; a continent that became the center of Christianity for two millennia. And to think it all started with a prayer by the river and a house church!

Apply

Is your house a church? Is it a spiritual center for the gospel in your area? What would need to be different for your house to be "worthy"?

Do

Have a discussion with your household (spouse, kids, roommates) about being a house church. What will you do so Jesus can use your spot on the map to reach the lost with the gospel? (Regular Bible talks, hospitality nights, family nights, devotional times and prayers?)

Yield

Lord, you've given me a place to live, help me use is to make my neighborhood alive for you...

Wednesday: Healing with the Word _____

Read
John 4:46-5:29

Examine

When the Word walked the earth, he had the power to heal. With a sentence Jesus could pronounce healing, cause the lame to walk and even raise the dead. When the Jewish leaders heard him say these things, they rightly devised that Jesus was putting himself on par with God. Only God could have such power in his words! But instead of falling before him in awe, they wrongly sought to put him to death for blaspheming their idea of God.

At the end of this passage Jesus talks about how people are marvelling at these healings but promises that we haven't seen anything yet. A time is coming when the dead will hear the voice of God and live. Later in John, Jesus' friend Lazarus experiences this very thing and the Jewish leaders just want Lazarus to die (again!). Of course, Jesus himself fulfills his own words by rising from the dead as a first fruit of the salvation to come.

Jesus walked around in a world filled with pain, brokenness, illness and death. So do we! He used his words to comfort those in pain, heal the broken and even raise the dead. He left us his word in the world so we could do the same! (John 14:12) When someone is struggling or hurting what do we do? The world offers little comfort or help but we have the word. We can pray and then lovingly comfort with the healing words of Jesus himself. We can even raise the dead by bringing words of life to friends and family. People think that sharing scripture is Bible bashing or holy rolling but it can just be encouraging if we share in a non-confrontational way with love in our hearts. The key is being filled up with God's word ourselves. Then we'll know just what to share and how to share it. You'll be amazed at what can happen when the Bible talks!

Apply
Who needs healing in your life? Who is broken down? Who may even be dying spiritually? Pray for them and for the Word to share that could heal them.

Do
Lovingly share a verse with a friend in need today.

Yield
Father, show me someone who needs your healing word today...

Thursday: Setting Captives Free _____

Read
Luke 4:16-30
John 8:30-59

Can you imagine being at Synagogue that day!? Jesus reads from Isaiah 61 and instead of some speech about how great it will be when the messiah comes to Israel he simply says, "Today this scripture has been fulfilled in your hearing." Then he just sits down. (The first century equivalent of a mic drop!) The people are amazed but then they start to question his authority because they believe they know who his "father" is. Jesus responds by reminding them of how God has a history of working with people outside of Israel when the people of Israel refuse to recognize what God is doing. They get so mad that they try to stone him but he simply walks through the crowd and leaves.

Twice in Jesus' mission statement from Isaiah 61 the word liberty is used. Jesus is proclaiming that his presence means that people who are held captive and oppressed will now have the opportunity to be freed. Apparently, nothing makes a person more angry than telling them that they are captives when they don't think they need to be freed. John 8 provides a similar (and hilarious) discussion with the same result. The Jewish leaders want to stone him to death on the spot! Interestingly, the question of freedom in both accounts seems to spark the question of who Jesus' father is. We should not be surprised because seeing God in the right way is our path to true freedom. The main function of the word is to show us who God is—thus "the truth will set us free".

When we think of the things that enslave us, (sin, addiction, pornography, substance abuse, and pride, to name a few) we often think of freeing ourselves by focusing on the problem. We want to overcome addiction by focusing on the addiction. But this usually only helps for a short time and we become more trapped and frustrated by the cycle of sin. Here's how the word of God is different and why it actually has the power to set the captives free: *Freedom doesn't come by focusing on what's oppressing us. It comes from focusing on the Father who loves us.* This is why the narrative in both of these passages goes from freedom to fatherhood. We're not enslaved by sin because of the sin alone. We're enslaved because we can't see God. Jesus (The Word) came to show us the Father and his love and in doing so to truly set the captives free.

Apply

Who do you know who is captivated by something other than God? How could showing them God—not focusing on their addiction/sin/character issue—help them become free? What scriptures would benefit someone who is struggling with addiction without addressing the addiction right away but by starting with a true picture of God?

Do

Pray and share God's word with a sin-captive in your life. Think about a passage that will show them who their Father in heaven is and how much he loves them. In order to do this you may need to start with yourself if you've forgotten the Father's love and become captivated by some other god.

Yield

Lord, let me use your word to set the captives free...

Friday: The Blind Will See _____

Read

Luke 4:18-19
John 9
2 Corinthians 4:1-6
Revelation 3:14-20

Examine

Spiritual blindness is a big problem but Jesus is an even bigger savior. His words were powerful enough to heal blindness and his word can still bring recovery of sight to the spiritually blind in our world today. My daughter, Genevieve, went through a phase where she would try to walk around the house with her eyes closed. She wouldn't make it very far before getting nervous and opening her eyes or running into something with her hands out to prevent injury. When I imagine what it would be like to be blind, it breaks my heart. People who are blind today have many resources and aids from enhanced crosswalks and audio resources to seeing-eye dogs and braille in public places. The visually impaired know that they need these helps to live.

The difference with the spiritually blind is that they often don't even know they are blind. The pharisees in John 9 and the Christians in Laodicea are good examples. They thought they could see. They thought their vision of God and his kingdom was clear. But Jesus declares them blind. What danger we face when we think we can see but we're really just stumbling through life!

As hometown missionaries we have the ability through the word of life to give sight to the blind. But our first task is often to show people that their vision needs correcting. Jesus does this bluntly and there may be situations where we need to employ this same kind of real talk but there is another way to help those who are stuck in spiritual darkness: shine the light!

When we share the word in a Bible talk or Bible study or even just in the course of conversation, we must stop sharing it dimly. Many of us have studied the same scriptures about the word of God or discipleship with different people over the years. We may have shared these passages a hundred times but the person we are sharing with may be hearing it for the very first time. Are we sharing with the excitement and joy that we should? Imagine someone who is blind getting to see for the first time. That's what's happening on the other side of the Bible study. Let's share with enthusiasm and zeal every single time! People don't like hearing that they are blind so don't start by telling them about blindness. Instead share the word without blandness! Open their eyes to the greatness of your God and the light will dawn in their hearts and show them what they've been missing!

Apply

Who is blind to God but doesn't realize it in your life? What passages could you share that might shine a great light on who God is and how much he loves them?

Do

Pray for someone who needs to see God. Powerfully and passionately share a passage about God that will inspire them. I love sharing the 3 parables of Luke 15 or the whole story of the world in just one parable (Matthew 21:33-46 The Parable of the Tenants).

Yield

Lord, shine through me by the power of your word so that the blind may see...

Saturday: The Year of the Lord's Favor _____

Read

Luke 4:18-19 (One more time!)
Leviticus 25:1-22

Examine

Jesus finishes his mission statement from Isaiah 61 by promising that his presence is a proclamation of "the year of the Lord's favor". This is likely a reference to the year of Jubilee that is spelled out in Leviticus 25. Seven was an important number for Israel. The seventh day was the Sabbath day of rest. The seventh year was an entire year of rest. Food would be stored up so that the whole nation could take a year off and allow the people, animals and land to rest in God. The year after 7 Sabbath years was to be the year of Jubilee. Thus, every 50 years everything in Israel would be reset. If you had fallen on hard times and had to sell some of your land, you would get it back (the original sale price would have been based on how many years were left until the next Jubilee). If you really had fallen on hard times and had to sell yourself to become an indentured servant, you would be freed. Every 50 years everything would be made right! What an amazing plan! Sadly, we have no scriptural record of the Jubilee year actually being practiced.

This makes Jesus' proclamation in the Synagogue that day all the more amazing. He's saying that his presence is Jubilee. He is the reset that will make everything right again. All the ways we've sold ourselves to sin and broken faith will be restored. He's the seventh seven who's come to restore all things!

Even with such a proclamation Jesus walked around in a world of darkness and brokenness and it killed him. And we walk in that same dark and broken world. But because of Jesus we can proclaim the Lord's favor in the darkness. We can preach Jubilee among the broken. The reason Israel may have never celebrated Jubilee is that it would take so much faith. The 49th year was a Sabbath and to have the 50th year also be a Sabbath meant that there would be no farming or work done for two whole years. To give back land or let servants go would be so difficult. All of these things would take massive trust in God. Faith is at the heart of Jubilee. Faith is key to living in the year of the Lord's favor. The faithful can walk around in the joy of the Lord even in the pain that surrounds us. And our faith can proclaim an alternative to the lostness that we see: a reset and restoration by the power of Jesus Christ and his word!

Apply

Who in your life needs a reset? Who needs restoration or a new start? You can proclaim the year of the Lord's favor to them by sharing the word of God.

Do

Share the word of God with jubilance! Pray for the best scriptures to share that will give someone faith that they can start fresh (Lamentations 3:22-24, 2 Corinthians 5:17 or Revelation 21:1-6 maybe?).

Yield

God, help my life to be a faith-filled jubilee as I share your word with joy...

Section 3: Hands

"But taking her by the hand he called, saying, 'Child, arise.'"

—Luke 8:54

Our hearts are changing, our feet are getting worn out, but the people we are reaching out to need more than a message. They need a hand. God's plan in Jesus Christ was to close the distance between himself and his people. And O how he closed that gap! In Jesus, God was no longer a terrifying voice heard from on high but a person just like us. As a person (who was also fully God), Jesus could have acted high and mighty. But instead he was as personal as can be. He touched the people that he interacted with, placing his hands on their wounds, helping them to stand up and making sure they knew that he cared deeply for them.

In this last section, we'll focus on touching people with the same love that Jesus showed. We're going to keep sharing our faith but we're going to really dial in on the heart that it takes to not just go through the motions. God doesn't need evangelism robots. He needs disciples that are willing to reach down and give a hand to those who are hurting; to pull them up so they can experience the loving relationship that Jesus stretched out his hands to secure on the cross.

In just a few weeks your training will be complete and there will be so much to celebrate. You may be celebrating a new brother or sister in Christ or maybe you'll still be searching for that open heart in your hometown. Ultimately, the result that matters most is your heart, feet and hands. If you allow them to be pierced and changed by the reading and challenges ahead, then you'll truly become the light your hometown needs. After all, Jesus shared his faith with us through the piercing of his heart, feet and hands. Being a hometown missionary is as simple and as difficult as following him to the cross and letting yourself be pierced too.

Week 9: The Least of These

"And the King will answer them, 'Truly, I say to you, as you did it to one of the least of these my brothers, you did it to me.'"

—Matthew 25:40

Of all the chapters in this book, I write this from the greatest place of personal weakness. It's not that I haven't had opportunities to serve vulnerable populations. I've served in multiple orphanages around the world through *HOPE worldwide*. I met my wife doing volunteer literacy work at a local elementary school. I've had moments of imitating Jesus' heart for the needy but this is far from a lifestyle. I wish I could skip this chapter altogether but such an omission would defy the very heart of God, displayed in Jesus Christ, as so much of his hometown mission was fulfilled in the lives of hurting people. I can't change the gospel to make it look more like my life but I pray that even in writing this chapter, my life will be changed by the gospel.

Are you a sheep or goat? **Read Matthew 25:31-46**

There's something compelling about the scribbled cardboard signs that beggars hold up at intersections. The back of a pizza box and some permanent marker are often the most convicting thing we read in a day. "Two hungry kids at home... army vet... anything helps... God bless..." One day I drove past a man holding a sign that simply said "Whatever you have done for the least of these, you have done for me." My heart burned within me as I read Jesus' words on his sign. I scrounged my car for change, for a stray granola bar, for anything, but I had nothing. I drove past but my conscience haunted me. I rolled through a fast food place and circled back. He was gone. I felt like I missed an opportunity to serve Jesus himself because I wasn't prepared. Since then, I've tried to keep something in my car to give to those in need but I'm still more goat than sheep.

Which side do you think you'll fall on when Jesus comes back? Let's break down this hard to swallow parable. Our hands are often empty because of our hearts. We could give but we choose not to and we rationalize it. We question what the person may spend our money on. We wonder how they got into such a situation. Must be poor choices! Addiction! Why can't they pull themselves up by the bootstraps? They aren't worthy of my money. Feel free to add your own thoughts as to why it's okay to withhold from the needy.

This parable cuts across each and every possible excuse we could make: when you withhold from the needy, you withhold from Jesus. None of our rationalizations work when we see the needy man or woman as Jesus himself. It doesn't matter how the money will be used or how the person got into such a situation. It's Jesus holding that sign, laying in the hospital, sitting in a cell, sleeping under a bridge or wondering where his next meal will come from. It's Jesus we are serving. Is he worthy of our help? It took a man holding up the very words of Jesus from this parable to shock my goatish heart. That's what Jesus' words do. He came to change our hearts regarding the needy. Have you been listening? Or rather, can you see?

> *Jesus knew that we don't just need a change of behavior but new eyes and a new heart.*

In order for us to be sheep and not goats we need to see the world the way he saw the world. Living like a goat makes so much sense through worldly eyes. It's hard to see any other way. The goat people couldn't even see Jesus because their mindset was so far from his. Yet, the sheep people see Jesus everywhere in everyone. Jesus wants to change our hearts so we can see him in the places we would least expect which happen to be the places he loved to hang out.

He ate (and drank) with sinners, befriended the lowest outcasts and enemies of the people, touched the untouchable and pardoned the unforgivable. Even his disciples (who were by no means the cream of the crop) had a hard time grasping this upside down messiah, just as we do today. Jesus explained the worldview that leads to the sheep side of life as he asked the same question to two people who were acting like goats and one blind sheep.

> *The question that Jesus asked both parties was simply, "What do you want me to do for you?"*

Read Mark 10:35-45

First James and John, the sons of thunder, who rightly believed that Jesus could call down fire from heaven to destroy faithless cities but wrongly believed that he should. So bold! They demand of Jesus to do their will and Jesus in such remarkable humility asks, "What do you want me to do for you?" One of us on your right and one on your left—no word on who sits where but I'm sure that would be the next dispute (Goats are never happy no matter how great their position). Jesus answers them compassionately, focusing at first on the ignorance of their question instead of the arrogance. "You don't know what you are asking." The other disciples hear about this and are indignant. Jesus uses the incident as an opportunity to teach as he so often did. He explains his worldview, our worldview as his disciples, *"Whoever would be great among you must be your servant, and whoever would be first among you must be slave of all. For even the Son of Man came not to be served but to serve, and to give his life as a ransom for many."*

Jesus not only taught this upside down vision of power, he lived and died it. When we are trying to be great, first, best, more comfortable, less inconvenienced, we won't see Jesus in all the great people he has surrounded us with. Our worldview blinds us to the reality that we get to serve Christ every time we see a person in need. This goes beyond the beggar on the corner. Jesus is the mentally ill person in the fellowship. He's the friend who keeps making bad financial choices. He's the oldest person in your church that you have nothing in common with and he's the youngest baby who won't stop crying during communion. He's every vulnerable soul that makes you feel uncomfortable. He's every conversation that you think people are judging you for having (Is she friends with her?). How many times did you see Jesus this week? Or are you having trouble seeing Jesus?

Read on in Mark 10:46-52

In contrast to the disciples who thought they could see Jesus clearly as they walked and talked with him and asked him ridiculous questions, we meet Bartimaeus, a blind beggar. He's crying out for Jesus, begging for mercy. Close your eyes for a moment and imagine the scene. Can you hear him crying out? And the crowd shushing him. The crowd, the world, and often Christians, always want to silence the needy. Want them to be invisible. They make us uncomfortable in their vulnerability. But there will always be needy among us. We can't silence them or make them invisible so we become blind and deaf to their cries. Our worldview doesn't include them in our field of vision. We give on our terms. Maybe we give at church when called upon.

> *Jesus refused to be blind and deaf to the cries of the blind and deaf or anyone with needs.*

He calls Bartimaeus to come to him and the blind man throws his cloak on the ground and springs up to meet Jesus. Jesus has a question for him, "What do you want me to do for you?" I wonder what James and John thought when they heard Jesus ask the very same question he had asked them! "Let me recover my sight." Jesus healed the blind man. He granted the request. And Bartimaeus became a follower of Christ. Same question, two very different outcomes.

Jesus has a question for you too. I'm sure you can guess what it is: "What do you want me to do for you?" Think about it. This isn't a genie in the bottle, three wishes, or anything like that but we have a savior who hears us and answers our prayers. What do you want Jesus to do for you? Make a list if you want. He will listen to each and every request. But he'll only grant those that align with his will. The way we answer this question reveals our hearts. Goat hearts or sheep hearts? So take a moment and really think and pray about this.

> *Imagine Jesus looking in your eyes and asking want you want from him. Answer the question. Write down your requests. Don't read on until you've done this.*

Are you a sheep or a goat? Do you see the world through the eyes of Christ or the eyes of the crowd? Examine your requests. Here's the litmus test: if Jesus were to answer your requests would you become greater or would others become greater? Would you have more (not just more stuff but more anything) or would you have more of Him and maybe less of other things? Who would benefit most from your request? You and your family or others? What do think? Would Jesus grant your request? Are you a sheep or a goat?

To be honest, my requests are usually a bit of both. I usually want this or that so I can help this person or that situation. My heart wavers between sheep and goat. Regardless of what you asked of Jesus I want you to ask this along with me: "Let me recover my sight." Help me to see you Jesus in every person I see. The Bartimaeus question may be the very best question we could ask of Jesus. After all, we know he's inclined to answer it! Recovery of sight—we aren't born blind to the needs of others. Children seem to innately desire to help others and sacrifice. No wonder Jesus said the kingdom belongs to them! We gradually lose sight of the needs of others as we get older and focus more and more on our own needs. We need recovery of sight, restoration of childlike hearts. Then we can look up to Jesus and honor the needy in our lives with loving service instead of looking down on them or not even seeing them at all. Bartimaeus asked to see and guess what he saw first when his eyes were opened? He saw Jesus.

In this week's devotionals we'll ask to see Jesus in the vulnerable people that we are so often blind to. We'll ask to hear his voice in the voices of those in need on our streets and in our churches. Hopefully, we'll come out of it a little more sheepish and a lot less goaty!

Week 9: In the Field Training

Peek at the Week

This week is all about seeing and serving Jesus in the people that need our love the most. John the baptist had the eyes of a sheep. Out of all the people who came to him to be baptized on the other side of the Jordan, he could see that the carpenter's son was the lamb of God. And he knew just what to do when he saw Jesus. "He must become greater, I must become less." That's the response of a person who truly sees Jesus. We can securely become the least of these because we rest in the greatness of our humble savior. Are you ready to have your eyes opened? An amazing thing happens when our eyes are opened to seeing Jesus in the needy people all around us: our hands open too. Our fists unclench and we begin to give cheerfully. Perhaps even more amazing, we start to see ourselves through the eyes of Jesus too. We are so needy! And only he can meet our every need. **No hashtags this week as we need to give in secret so that we will be blessed by God and our hearts will stay pure.**

Family Challenge and Activity

This week you are going to give yourself away in a creative manner of your choosing. It takes intentionality and effort. You got this! **Pick from one of these** and apply yourself to the daily challenges so you can become less by making others (and ultimately Jesus) greater. With your family or friends gather and:

- Make a give away bag for your car. Stock a bag or box with imperishable snacks and drinks so you can give to those who have need on your commute. It doesn't have to be elaborate. It just needs to be prepared so you'll be prepared to give to Jesus as he begs on the roadside or at the park.

- Make a random encouragement card for a brother or sister at church. In the parable of the sheep and goats Jesus says, whatever you did for the "least of these my brothers." So we must lookout for the needy in our churches. You might know of a need that you can encourage with a card or you might not. Pray for the Spirit to lead you to write a randomly encouraging note and to show you who needs it at the next worship service.

If you are reading this book with your church look out for a church wide service event and plan on giving your whole heart.

Monday: Pure and Undefiled Religion _____

Read
James 1:27-2:17

Examine

Jesus' brother does not mince words as he challenges the early church to see people without partiality. What a challenge! Contrary to the popular saying, we always judge books by their covers and we make judgments about people within moments of meeting them (or even before we meet them). Since this is our nature, James rightly counsels us to be impartial in our judgments. We're going to judge—it's what we do with it that makes the difference.

Do we honor those who are well off in the world's eyes or do we honor those parts that seem to be weaker? In most of our hometowns there are not orphanages. In America, widows are likely to be taken care of by social security. Maybe we wonder how we can even practice this "pure and undefiled" religion that James speaks of. We just need to look around in our own fellowship with the eyes of Christ. We'll see children who desperately need love and care. The elderly will become visible instead of sitting quietly in the background. You're probably thinking of some vulnerable people in your fellowship or in your neighborhood right now. Seeing the need is the first step. But what do we do next? James gives us insight in today's text.

Give them your attention. Show them that you value them. Yes, you've judged them—we all do. And because of Christ you've judged them as worthy of your time, conversation, or a listening ear. Change the way you operate at church. We can be so selfish with our agendas as we navigate the fellowship. Let the Spirit lead you to what he values. Let him lead you to Jesus who lives in the oldest and youngest among us. You'll get way more than you give anyway!

Apply

What if you changed the way you fellowship? What if you prayed before you came to church to see what Jesus would have you see and to serve those in need instead of meeting your own needs? Now imagine if the whole church did this? How gloriously different would the fellowship look, feel and even sound?

Do

Pray before you go to church about seeing Jesus everywhere and in everyone. Pray as you walk through the fellowship to see Jesus and not leave him hanging.

Yield

Jesus, help me to see your face among the saints...

Tuesday: Mission and Money _____

Read

2 Corinthians 9:6-15

Examine

God doesn't need our money to complete his mission, but it sure helps! And it always has. When you think about the ways you spend money, do you spend money like a missionary? Is part of your income devoted to tithing so your hometown can be reached? Do you give to foreign missions and aid organizations so that the whole world can be reached? I wonder what Paul would counsel me to do if I showed him my bank account!

More important than what we give to the needy locally and far away are our hearts as we give. Paul makes it clear that we must give what we've decided, without reluctance or compulsion. This takes prayer and forethought. It's not just participating in a church giving campaign or dropping pocket change in the offering. God can use our hard earned money, cheerfully given, to reach people with the gospel. What better use of our money is there?

Apply

Does your budget reflect your faith and mission? How does God use money to help save souls? Is there any way that you could give more to support the mission at home and abroad?

Do

Go through your finances with a missionary mindset. Decide to give as much as you can to the mission.

Yield

Lord, you're the true source of my wealth, show me how I can give back...

Wednesday: Opportunity _____

Read

Philippians 4:10-20

Examine

What do you think of when you hear the word opportunity? A promotion or a raise? A chance to take a vacation? Paul praises the Philippians for sharing in his troubles as soon as an opportunity presented itself. When we see someone hurting or struggling with a sin, do we see this as an opportunity? Are we eager to jump into their brokenness and be allies? As we begin to see Jesus in the needy, we begin to see hardships as opportunities to serve king and kingdom.

The way that Paul speaks takes the pressure off. We don't meet people's needs. That's God's job. He strengthens. Sometimes we balk at serving because we feel under-qualified or under-resourced (inadequate) to help. The Lord is our helper, we shall not be in want. When we step into an opportunity with loving servants hearts, we should feel joy and not pressure. God's got this! In fact, as we give of ourselves and serve, God will supply our needs too.

Apply

If you think about it, you are probably surrounded by opportunities to serve and love people with all kinds of needs. What's holding you back from giving to those who have a need? How can you enter into the needs of others with the expectation that God will provide?

Do

Make a list of some needs you see around you. Don't worry about how to meet those needs. Just recognize the needy, pray for them and pray for the Spirit to lead.

Yield

Lord, let me see the needy as opportunities to unleash your goodness....

Thursday: Effectiveness

Read

2 Peter 1:3-11

Examine

Have you ever noticed that the things we are to add to our character go from inward focused to outward focused? Faith, virtue, knowledge, self-control, steadfastness and godliness are by no means individual pursuits. We need the kingdom if we are to increase in these. But these first virtues are concerned with our characters. The last two virtues are concerned with others: brotherly affection and love. I don't think the order of these disciplines is a coincidence. We do not grow in Christ just so we can be better. Our ultimate goal is to love one another, showing ourselves to be true disciples.

Peter goes on to teach that when we increase in these qualities, then we can consider ourselves effective and fruitful. Conversely, if we lack in these we are blind, forgetting that we have been forgiven of such a great sin debt. Just like the word opportunity, it is easy for us to allow the world to define the word effective. A worldly idea of effectiveness even slips into our churches, especially as we focus on the mission. Effectiveness is not measured by baptisms, or tithes, or salaries, or promotions. Effectiveness is measured by virtue piled upon virtue with brotherly affection and love at the top of the heap.

Apply

How do you view being effective? When we see this word through Peter's eyes we are granted a freedom to love those who need love and affection without an agenda. The effective Christ follower aims to be as loving as possible to as many as possible so that God can cause fruit to grow.

Do

Have the most effective day of your life. Abandon your agenda and decide to be the most loving person that you know for one day.

Yield

Father, make me an effective Christ follower... increase my affection and love for others...

Friday: With (How to be with someone) _____

Read

John 1:35-42

Examine

Oftentimes we don't help because we don't know how to help. We see those in need but when we think of what to do for them we're at a loss. Maybe we even think we'll make matters worse by trying to help. If you've struggled with thoughts like these, then I've got great news for you. You probably don't need to do anything at all. It's often not about our actions but simply our presence.

Look at how Jesus ministered to these men who would one day change the world. No lessons, no miracles, not even a prayer is recorded. "They stayed with him." Do you know how powerful it is to just be with someone? You can say it like Jonathan's armor bearer famously declared, *"I am with your heart and soul"* (1 Samuel 14:7). But what really counts is what you do next. The armor bearer followed up his words by climbing right behind Jonathan and entering the seemingly impossible fight with him. God blessed and they won the victory!

Of course God loves it when we're with one one another. The Bible, from cover to cover, explains how God is doing everything he can to be with us again like he was in the garden. From tabernacle to temple, incarnation to indwelling, redemption to restoration, God just wants to be with us.

Apply

Is there someone in your life that needs you to simply be with them? How could your loving presence begin to make a difference? Are you lonely? Do you need someone to be your partner through hardship? It takes so much vulnerability to ask for someone to be with you but it may be the difference between staying faithful and falling away.

Do

Pick a person to be with. Again, don't expect yourself to meet needs. Just offer your presence and deliver. Be open to the Spirit and watch what God can do.

Yield

Lord help me to be with someone in the same way that you are with me...

Saturday: Bruised Reed, Smoldering Wick _____

Read
Matthew 12:15-21

Examine

Matthew sees Jesus as the embodiment of the messiah that Isaiah foresaw. In this description we get a glimpse of how Jesus was when he healed and ministered. Have you ever wondered what a healing encounter with Jesus would be like? What impression would he leave on a crowd? Meditate on verse 20. Jesus was gentle with the vulnerable and hurting. If a reed was already bruised, he would make sure it didn't break. There's no adding insult to injury, just healing and grace. If a wick was about to burn out, he wouldn't provide the final blow. On the contrary he would fan the flame so it could burn brightly again. This was the expectation Isaiah gave us of Jesus. And this was exactly how Jesus walked among the people. How do we conduct ourselves as his hometown missionaries?

So often we want "problems" to go away. In our sinful hearts that can include people whose sin or affliction negatively affect us. Jesus' example teaches us to be gentle with those who are hurting. Even the most damaged reed or faintest flame should be uplifted in our presence and not shot down. Isn't this how we would want to be treated when our wounds get exposed and our lights grow dim?

Apply

Who is bruised among you? Whose light has begun to fade? If you're honest, who would make your life easier if they just went away? These are exactly the people that we need in our lives if we are to become gentle like Jesus.

Do

Decide to be gentle to the hurting all around you. Choose compassion over criticism no matter what.

Yield

Lord, may I give you the patience and gentleness of Christ in all my relationships...

Week 10: The Harvest is Plentiful

"The harvest is plentiful..."

Jesus says this a few times, go ahead and read them for yourself.

Read Matthew 9:35-38, Luke 10:1-3, John 4:27-38

In Matthew, before Jesus appoints any disciples/missionaries, he himself goes to the towns and villages proclaiming the gospel. He has compassion because he sees them as harassed and helpless, sheep without a shepherd. Then he calls the disciples to himself and tells them the harvest is plentiful but the workers are few. God is the Lord of the harvest and we are to pray to him earnestly for more laborers. The grain is ripe, but it's dying on the plant because there are not enough workers.

In Luke, as Jesus sends out the 72 2x2 he repeats what he had told the twelve disciples a chapter earlier. Their mission in each town is to find more missionaries, not just make believers but make disciples who will make disciples.

The circumstance in John is quite different, but the message is the same. The disciples are freaking out because Jesus is talking to a woman, and worse a Samaritan woman! It's such a cultural taboo that they wonder if maybe he's lightheaded from not eating. But Jesus came to challenge cultural norms. He explains that in the world of agriculture we wait for the harvest (it would be 4 months from sowing to reaping for wheat and barley which look white on a sunny day near harvest time) but in God's eyes the fields are ready and the harvest of eternal life has begun. They should see themselves as those tasked with collecting a crop that they did not plant. God has been planting seeds and now that Jesus is on the earth the harvest can begin.

There are so many allusions to agriculture in the scriptures. The world in the time of Jesus was largely agrarian, with the people of Israel being mostly farmers and shepherds. Most of us are a little more removed from farming these days. I'm afraid that my kids don't know what an actual carrot looks like. But we still understand the timeless language of agriculture. This is one of the ways that the Spirit worked to keep the Bible relevant for all time. As long as human beings eat, stories about crops and herds will make sense!

> *So Jesus' message to his disciples is simple: "The harvest is plentiful."*

This immediately destroys any excuse that might keep us from sharing our faith like: "No one is open." "No one at my work wants to hear about God." "Our society is becoming more secular and people don't respond to God like they used to." I could go on because I've thought all of those things myself but you get the point. Jesus has a big red rubber stamp for all of those logical sounding excuses. THE HARVEST IS PLENTIFUL. The fields are ripe!

Let's take a deep dive into this metaphor and try to understand what it means to look at those sheep without a shepherd as a harvest. A harvest is a time of gathering when the crop is ripe. We'll look at both aspects: ripeness and the time of gathering.

Harvest Time All The Time
Read Ecclesiastes 3:1-11

For everything there is a season. We see this in agriculture as it says in verse 2, *"A time to plant and a time to pluck up what has been planted."* We see this in every part of our lives as well. We have seasons of education, career, retirement. Seasons of health, illness, injury. Seasons of singleness, marriage, child rearing, empty nesting. But there is one thing that the writer says does not have a season: Eternity. Verse 11 tells us that *"God makes everything beautiful in its time but he has put eternity in our hearts causing us to wonder at the work of God from beginning to end."* In other words, it's always time for eternity. There's no season where our hearts and the hearts of every person don't long for something more, something that will last forever, something that will break the cycle of these temporary seasons that we find ourselves drifting in and out of.

Eternity is not seasonal—by definition—it's eternal! Jesus knew this and so he could talk about it being harvest time with his disciples when it was still planting time. Four months out, the fields were still dirt, certainly not "white for the harvest" and yet Jesus could proclaim that the harvest is ready. He makes the point in an even more radical way as he is coming and going from Jerusalem near the end of his life: You need to read this crazy story: **Mark 11:12-14** and **Mark 11:20-26**.

It almost seems cruel that Jesus would curse a fig tree for not having figs when it wasn't even the season for figs—I've always kind of felt bad for that tree! But here's how it also makes sense:

> *Jesus had a ridiculous expectation of ripeness. With the presence of Jesus it is always harvest time. There should be fruit on the tree because Jesus is there.*

We have the presence of Jesus. He tells us to pray and not doubt that the harvest is plentiful, that people will be open, that they will respond to Jesus and the gospel. What if instead of doubting that anyone would ever say yes to our invitation to church or a Bible study, we took Jesus at his word that the harvest is plentiful? What if we shared his radical expectation of ripeness?

This is crucial because here's what's happening when we doubt that people will be open: Who plants the seed of eternity in people's hearts? Who is the sower? It's God! And who tells us repeatedly (in each of the gospels) to expect a harvest? Jesus! So we might think we're doubting ourselves or our ability to be bold or to share the scriptures effectively but we're really just doubting the power of God and the promises of Jesus! So Jesus says, as he stands next to a withered fig tree, "have faith in God!"

> *God is readying souls for the harvest and the presence of Jesus makes the fields ripe. You just need to bring the presence of Jesus and watch what God does!*

Now, we know from experience that not everyone that we ask says yes to Jesus on the first invitation. But a farmer doesn't give up on his crop because it's not ready the first time he checks on it. He keeps watering it and fertilizing it (loving it) until it's ripe. If we really believe that the harvest is plentiful we'll have the patience to endure with our friends as the Spirit continues to work on their hearts. They will be ready. Will you still be waiting and praying earnestly for their eternity?

I think the challenge here is to keep ourselves from getting stuck in the seasons of life that are temporary but seem all important at the time. Your marriage, your kids, your education, your career, your health—those are all seasonal—they are subject to change and they are limited to this life. What if we recognized those seasons and honored those seasons but didn't allow ourselves to be consumed by them? What if we lived on a deeper plane with our hearts set on the one thing that never goes out of season—eternity? How differently would we approach all of those other seasons of life if we didn't lose sight of eternal life? How much more joy would we live with? How much less anxiety from moment to moment? How much more impact through all the seasons? "In season and out of season" we'd be prepared to preach the word as Paul urged Timothy (2 Timothy 4:1-2).

Imagine as fall comes around and you're walking in woods as the leaves are falling but there's one tree that never loses its leaves and all winter long it flowers and bears fruit. That would be something to marvel at! With Christ, we can remove ourselves from the cycles of the seasons and live with an eternal perspective even before eternity is ushered in. We can be something to marvel at!

Harvest Time at the End of Time

Speaking of eternity, in agriculture, harvesting is not a continual activity. THE harvest is an event in which the crop is gathered all at once. Because of the presence of Jesus through the Holy Spirit it is always harvest time. But we also look forward to THE harvest to come when Jesus returns. We're 10 chapters into our training and guess what? It's time for a little fire and brimstone. Buckle up!

Check out Matthew 13:24-30 and the explanation in 13:36-43

This parable seems easy enough to understand but the disciples have a hard time with it so it is one of two parables that Jesus explains, leaving us little room to guess. The other one he explains is also about the harvest, the parable of the sower that we talked about a couple of chapters ago.

Did you read Jesus' explanation of the parable? I have to admit that's not exactly how I would have interpreted that parable! It's interesting to me that the angels are the reapers. What a great reminder that as we share our faith and study the Bible with people and see people baptized, it's not about us! We couldn't do this without the angels! How often do we think about that?

Overall, Jesus is very clear: the final harvest has been delayed so that it will be easy to discern the wheat from the weeds. Ouch! If you've ever wondered why this world is so messed up or been shocked by a headline or indignant about something terrible happening in your life, here's God's answer: the world is full of weeds. A lot of people want to blame God for the hurt in this world but in our free will we allow evil to get in and grow like crazy in our hearts and spread all over God's good earth. And the only reason we keep seeing such evil is because God is patient, not wanting anyone to perish, but everyone to come to repentance (2 Peter 3:8-9). He's giving the weeds a chance to become wheat before the angels come back to make things right.

I've learned a lot and been very convicted myself as I've written these lessons and training. This is an area where I felt like God punched me in the gut as this conviction dawned on me: I've practically stopped believing in hell. Theologically and in my mind I never stopped believing that there will be judgment and some people will get to be with God forever and others will not. But my actions (even as an evangelist) tell a different story from my beliefs. There is a lack of congruency.

If I really believe that people that I love will not be in eternity with God, then why do I lack urgency to share with them about Jesus? If I really believe this person God has placed in my life is going to meet Jesus at the end of their life then why wouldn't I try my hardest to introduce them to Jesus before that day comes? If I really believe that falling in love with God and the church and learning what it means to make Jesus Lord through studying the Bible leads to eternity then would I, as far as it is up to me, study the Bible with someone once every few weeks, taking months for them to get baptized? That's the culture I've fostered in our church.

Brother, sister, have you stopped believing in hell? Have you begun to worship the false idol of an all loving God, an all merciful God, who is not also just and righteous and true? Don't answer with your theological beliefs, answer with your life.

Maybe this is all a little too fire and brimstone for you. Let me remind you that Jesus brought it up! Maybe you're a more positive person—okay—do you really believe in heaven? Do you believe that this entire life is just a season and true life that never ends, life with God, is on the horizon? Do you want that eternity just for yourself or do you want everyone to be with God when he comes back to judge the living and the dead?

In our church we had a gospel night on a Friday. (If your church is doing this book, yours might be coming up!) In the old days it would be called a harvest night or a chariot ride—like when the chariots of fire came and picked up Elijah. It might have been called a revival meeting 100 years ago. A tent would be set up outside of town and people would bring their friends and sit them in the front row which was called the mourners bench. Down in the Bible belt it would be hot in that tent and the preacher would be yelling and spitting hellfire right on top of these people and at the end of a long message about the fires of hell the preacher would ask who wants to be saved and the people in the front would shoot up their hands. They'd come up and pray and be instructed to study the Bible and find a church and get baptized. All of that got short-cutted into altar calls and praying Jesus into your heart and other doctrines and practices that aren't actually in the Bible if you've ever wondered how churches started doing those things.

Now, our gospel night wasn't hellfire and brimstone but it did tap into the eternal. We talked about something that we should talk about all the time but we rarely do: "How's your soul doing?" (The conversation can be found in Appendix C on page 242). I want you to think about your friends, on whom Jesus would have compassion and say they are sheep without a shepherd but the harvest is plentiful. He believes in the harvest no matter what things look like on the outside and he wants everyone to be saved.

You can have an eternity driven soul talk with them that changes their lives literally forever. All you have to do is pray for the people that God has placed on your heart, and initiate a hard conversation. Will you be urgent for your friend? Will you believe in eternity for those who are stuck in the here and now? Will you give someone the opportunity to learn that they are more than just a bag of bones—they are a soul built for eternal life with God?

I'll end this chapter with my favorite parable. One more farming story from Jesus that happens to put the entire history of the world—past, present and future— into perspective in just a handful of verses.

Read the Parable of the Tenants: Matthew 21:33-46

This is so amazing. Jesus talks about the creation of the world and God's special people Israel as this vineyard that wasn't accidentally created but lovingly made with a watchtower and a winepress and a wall. And it's not a place without purpose, but it's been given to us so that we would produce something with our lives in God's vineyard. Just as a vineyard has the purpose of producing wine, our lives should produce amazing things for God! We've been lovingly placed in God's creation with a purpose. Isn't it cool that this farming story can tell us all of that?

We aren't just supposed to produce for ourselves, but for God. After all, it's his vineyard. He's expecting a harvest. But throughout history when God has sent messengers to remind his people of this they have beat them and even killed them. Jesus is speaking of the Old Testament prophets.

Then, in the most amazing twist, Jesus inserts himself into the story and explains what is going to happen to him before it even happens. God goes to the greatest lengths, even sending his own son to collect the harvest, but the wicked see this as an opportunity to have self rule so they take him and kill him outside of the vineyard. Sure enough, Jesus would be crucified outside of the city of Jerusalem soon after. He puts it on his audience to decide what should happen to such a person who would kill the master's son in order to gain power.

Then he quotes the very messianic Psalm 118 to drive home his point:

"The stone the builders rejected has become the cornerstone."

Picture this verse. It's as if all of our choices are before us. All the idols and gods of this world are like rocks in a quarry and in our free will as the builders of our lives we can examine each rock and decide if we'll make it our cornerstone. The charge Jesus makes here is that they have picked up the Rock that is Jesus Christ and they examined it and they have found it wanting. They rejected it and threw it down and kept looking for something to base their lives on. But God has taken this rejected stone and made it the cornerstone—the stone on which everything that matters in the kingdom of God will be built.

And then he gives them a choice:

> *You can fall on this stone and be broken or it can fall on you and you will be crushed.*

Making Jesus the Lord of your life, accepting the cornerstone, is not easy. It will break our family and our friends. It will break habits. It will break and smash idols. It will sometimes break relationships so God can rebuild better ones. Think about when you fell down before Jesus and made him Lord. What did God need to break down in your life so he could begin building your life in him?

> *We have a serious task as hometown missionaries: We get to help people become beautifully broken by God so he can rebuild them with Jesus Christ as the foundation—with eternal building blocks that will last forever.*

The alternative is that the rock falls on them and they are crushed. I know we don't want that for our friends and family. Jesus promises the religious people of that time that the kingdom will be taken from them and given to a people who will produce its fruit. They wanted to claim that they were God's people based on their heritage and their culture like many do still to this day. But God counts his people by those who produce his fruit.

The harvest is plentiful!

What will God produce through you?

What needs to be broken in you so you can bear even more fruit?

Who will hear the gospel because you truly believe in eternity?

The harvest is plentiful!

Week 10: In the Field Training

The harvest is plentiful! This week's devotionals are all about lessons we can learn from agricultural metaphors in the scriptures. I know that doesn't sound exciting but you'll be amazed at how God can make you grow when you dive into his word this week! (See what I did with that agricultural metaphor!) Agriculture depends on seasons and timing so we'll get a good dose of scriptures on God's timing and ours as we seek to be fruitful in season and out of season. This week's hashtags are obvious **#hometownmissionary #theharvestisplentiful.** Tell a faithful evangelism story or share a picture of a worship service, Bible study or gospel moment. **This week's challenge is to invite the three people you've been praying for to church or a Bible study or to your Gospel Night if your church is having one.** Make sure you're putting your Mission Moments on the Mission Map. It should be so inspiring to see how much impact you can have in your hometown with the visual of the Mission Map!

Gospel Night "How Is Your Soul Doing?"

● See Appendix C for details.

I am praying for and will invite:

1._____

2._____

3._____

At this point in your hometown missionary training, you've been sharing your faith, having Bible talks and Bible studies, and hosting hospitality times. *It's time to lovingly and passionately invite the people that we've shared with to come to church or study the Bible with us.* Remember, our experience teaches us that people make Jesus Lord when they learn the gospel, fall in love with God, and fall in love with the church. It takes all of us working together to help impact our family and friends! Fill your church with new faces in these last few weeks of Hometown Missionary training and set yourself up for a harvest.

Family Activity

Gather together for a meal. Before you eat spend time praying for all the people that you are reaching out to. Your food might start to get a little cold but it's a great reminder of all the people who are hungry for the gospel and starving for salvation in our hometowns. Family devotionals don't need to be elaborate. Talk about what you've been learning and who you're sharing with as you dig into your dinner.

Monday: Exposed—What are you living for? ___

Read

2 Peter 3:8-14

Hebrews 3:13, 10:25

Examine

God has many eternal, unending qualities. God is love and always will be. He will always be just. His patience, however, is not an eternal quality. God will stop waiting at some point in our future. Thus, the harvest is plentiful today. The time for patience and the opportunity for repentance will end and he will return. Peter tells us that God's understanding of time (which he created and exists independently of) is not like ours. In Hebrews, it's as if the writer has insight into God's calendar: "Today" is the day of salvation and God's tomorrow is the "Day" when he returns.

People have long wrestled with how much of the "fire and brimstone" is metaphorical and how much is literal. I don't think it matters if the fire is real. What matters is God's intention and the final result of his return. I think the keyword in this passage (which is also greatly debated) is at the end of verse 10: "exposed". At the dawn of God's tomorrow, all the things that we've lived for that seemed so important will be exposed for what they really are. If they are eternal, they will last but anything less than the eternal is like a flower in the field. It's so hard to see what we're truly living for day-to-day and season-to-season, but it will be so clear on that Day.

So Peter counsels his beloved and us to live lives for God now before that day comes. Set your hearts and lives on the eternal. That same word "exposed" is the word "found" in verse 14. We don't have to feel anxious or scared about what's coming next. We can look forward to life forever with God. We can be at peace because as the heavens and earth are exposed for what they really are, we will be found as sons and daughters of the living God.

God's heart is that every single person would live for eternity and be found in him. And he's entrusted us to work with the angels in this age of patience before our salvation is finally realized.

Apply

How will God use you in this day of salvation? How can you more intentionally work the fields that are ripe for the harvest before God returns?

Do

Share your faith with someone today. Most of the things we have to do in a day are temporary but sharing Jesus with a friend echoes into eternity.

Yield

Lord, may I and as many as possible that I know be found in you on that day...

Tuesday: A Purpose Behind the Pruning _____

Read

John 15:1-17

Examine

Why do we face times of struggle or suffering? When we're dealing with hardship, we often question ourselves and God. We wonder if we did anything to deserve this. We wonder why God would let this happen. In some of his last words before he died, Jesus promises us that God will prune us in order to make us more fruitful. Have you ever considered that God is not only allowing hardship in your life but causing it in order to give you an abundantly fruitful life? Some of the most fruitful times in my life were also the most difficult. One of the marks of true faith is bearing fruit in hard times.

I am trying to grow a small apple orchard and I'm getting help from a tree expert (thanks Jake!). I want apples as soon as possible but every time Jake comes to look at my trees he cuts them way down. He knows that it's more important for the tree to be strong in the roots where I can't even see growth and to have the right structure so it can support all the fruit that will come someday. We are not very different from the trees! We need to be pruned (sometimes painfully) in order to grow the unseen parts and support structures that can lead to a fruitful life. Trees rely on sun, water and nutrients to grow. We rely on God. And God will lovingly cut back the things in our lives that keep us from abiding in him.

There are many ways to be fruitful besides making disciples so we should not read "bearing fruit" to only mean baptizing people. However, in verse 16 Jesus says we are to "go and bear fruit" so there is a correlation between soul winning and bearing fruit. I guess it's obvious: a life abiding in God, connected to the vine and the vinedresser, will be a life of impact that far outlives our last breath.

Apply

Think about hard times you've experienced recently. Can you see how God could use those hardships to bring you closer to him and make you more fruitful? How does this perspective change the way you look back on your difficulty?

Do

Pray about your hardships with this pruning perspective. Share your faith today. Tell someone what you've been going through and how it can bring you closer to God.

Yield

Thank you God, for the hardships in my life, I want to use them to become fruitful...

Wednesday: Perspective on Production _____

Read

1 Corinthians 3:1-23

Examine

Whose job it is to grow people and make them ready for salvation? Is it yours? Is it the job of your evangelist, ministry staff or small group leader? We should hope not! If so, we are trying to do God's job or expecting people to do the work of God. That is not a position we should ever want to find ourselves or our churches in. God makes it grow! Like Paul and Apollos, we plant seeds and water by sharing our faith, loving, and encouraging people but only God makes people grow. God brings people salvation—only God.

This perspective is so important. Even as we focus so much on being hometown missionaries, we have to remember that it's his mission and that even the most fruitful among us are just doing our limited part. How easily do we, like the Corinthians, make fruitful people into giants of faith only to shrink God? Gratitude for the impact our spiritual heroes have had on our lives must ultimately be gratitude for God lest we remain human focused, spiritual infants.

At best we are God's field (an acre or two of dirt). We are God's farmhands, God's builders. Amen for the work that has been done and the work we are currently doing but it is all the work of God. When we start to take credit or give credit to people, then God goes to work at one of his other jobs: exposing hearts and revealing what has truly been built. Whatever was built by human hands won't last. Like a farmer trying to grow without sunlight or a builder building without an architect, producing fruit or building our church without God will end in disaster. God loves us too much to let it be any other way!

We don't need to worship people or fall for cults of personality that only divide and destroy. "All things are yours." God has blessed us beyond any one person by giving us everything that we need. "All are yours, and you are Christ's, and Christ is God's."

Lastly, there are times when we share and love and encourage and we still don't see anyone coming to faith. This perspective on production is essential in such times. Don't get discouraged! Don't feel defeated. Don't try to be more "effective" or "successful." Just keep doing your part (planting seeds and watering) and God will do his in his perfect timing and perfect way. When we focus on ourselves we are quick to give up and get discouraged. When we focus on him, we will persevere and see how God always makes things grow!

Apply

How much of your faith is based on people? Think about the people who've impacted your life in Christ. Do you have a Godly perspective of their work in Christ or might you be setting people on pedestals?

Do

Don't shy away from sharing your faith for fear of being idolized. **Share about God today knowing that you are just a builder.**

Yield

God, help me to remember that you make things grow...

Thursday: Dying to Make Disciples

Read

John 12:12-25

Examine

The crowds declare Jesus king. The buzz about his power to even raise the dead is electric as his fame spreads throughout Jerusalem. Even non-Jews are seeking after him. How often do we long for such an open environment in the places we go? Open campuses, family members seeking after God, a workplace welcoming of the gospel—we pray for this! Jesus sees what is happening, but he also understands what it takes to bring salvation. He knows that salvation doesn't come from believing in the spectacle but from laying down one's life.

We see this same cycle of life in our world every year. The seeds must fall in autumn if we're going to see life in the spring. Imagine if one year all the plants held onto their seeds? Well that would be the end of life! The death life cycle is that important. Jesus needed to die so that we could be saved. The people calling him king and seeking after him only served to remind him of the real sacrifice that was soon going to be made.

This is gut-check time. What are we willing to give so that people can meet Jesus? We get so excited when someone seems open to the gospel but then reality sets in. They need so much love and encouragement and teaching! To do our small part in helping God do his great work to bring a soul from death to life we must give so much! Are you willing to drop whatever you need to in your life so that the gospel can be implanted and take root in the life of another? As followers of Jesus, who died so we could have salvation, we should expect to sacrifice as we live out our hometown mission. Sacrifice is what takes our faith and the budding faith of those God is using us to impact from surface level spectacle to the depth of discipleship that can truly change the world.

Apply

What sacrifice needs to be made for the lost in your life? How could you imitate your savior and lay your life down for another?

Do

Tell someone about Jesus today. Be willing to sacrifice your time, reputation, doubt, anything to be used by God to help someone connect to the cross of Christ.

Yield

Lord, show me what I need to lay down so you can build up others in my life...

Friday: God's Timing —Summer Time! _____

Read

Leviticus 23:23-44
1 Corinthians 15:50-58

1 Thessalonians 4:13-18

Examine

In a previous devotional we saw how Jesus' death and resurrection on Passover weekend and the inauguration of the kingdom of God 50 days later at the early harvest festival of Pentecost (feast of weeks) held great significance. As we continue to look at God's timing and passages about harvest, the Holy Days that follow Pentecost reveal what's next for our world.

If we look at the Jewish year as a microcosm of God's timeline, winter and spring have passed (Passover and Pentecost, crucifixion and the inauguration of the church). We are now in the summer with fall and the fall Holy Days on the horizon as we wait for the harvest to ripen. So what's next on God's calendar?

Well first comes the feast of trumpets. Trumpets were blown for many reasons: to signal an invasion, to herald the coming of a king, and to call people to worship. When Jesus comes back and the trumpet sounds, all of those things will ring true as heaven invades earth and we all worship king Jesus.

After the trumpet sounds, judgment comes. Judgment always has two sides. Some will be cut off from God while others will be atoned (literally "at oned" or made one with God). The great and dreadful day of the Lord will reveal those who are his.

Then comes the harvest and our new home with God. After the day of atonement the Jewish people celebrated the feast of booths or tabernacles. As the fields were harvested, they would make tents out of branches and leaves to eat and sleep in. I love being outside and it brings me joy to think that God had a week long national camp out built into Israel's Holy Days! But, if I'm honest, camping gets old pretty quick. The difference for us is that after atonement, the harvest will bring us not to a tabernacle of sticks and leaves but to permanent rest in God's eternal home.

So, now it's summer. This is the time of growth before the trumpet blows, before atonement is realized, and before the harvest is gathered to the eternal storehouses of God. Someday, in the blink of an eye, fall will come and harvest time will be upon us. Let's work the fields while we can!

Apply

Knowing that God's calendar is being fulfilled should fill us with faith and purpose. If the trumpet will soon sound then how should we live? What would it look like to live for eternity and not just for this world?

Do

Share your faith today while you still can. Think about the people that you want to spend eternity with and give them an opportunity to meet God before he returns at the trumpet blast on that day.

Yield

Lord, help me live in your timing, urgent for the harvest...

Saturday: Between The Trees

Read

Genesis 2:8-9
Isaiah 55:12-13
Galatians 3:13-14
Revelation 22:1-5

Examine

I go for prayer walks in the woods and I imagine the trees clapping their hands. On windy days they creak and moan but I've yet to hear clapping outside of my overactive imagination. The scriptures refer to trees more than we may realize. In fact, from beginning to end, trees play a central role in God's story. It all begins in the garden with the tree of life allowing mankind to live into eternity. But another tree, bearing the fruit of the tree of the knowledge of good and evil, brings sin and death because of disobedience to God. Later, Moses would declare in the law that anyone who dies on a tree is cursed. Thus, on the cross, Jesus willingly becomes a curse for us to remove the curse of sin that began back in the garden. And then the Bible concludes by painting a picture of eternity that is symbolized by a city with a river running through it and in which we find the tree of life always bearing fruit (That's a lot of Bible trees!).

We live between the trees of life; saved by Christ's death on a tree. Eternity surrounds us on all sides but like the flowers of the field or the trees of the forest, our lives here are not permanent. This lack of permanence should be enough to motivate us to live for something more. Yet, it seems our lives are just long enough to lull us into forgetting that we were built for something more; for the eternal.

When we walk through cemeteries (another place I love to pray) we see the years that people were born and when they died separated by a dash. That's it. A dash. A blink. That's all we've got here. We live in the dash between two numbers. But the scriptures, from beginning to end, teach us that our lives are actually much more than that. We don't just live between birthdate and death date. We live between the trees. We live a life that's destined to end with a meeting between heaven and earth; between us and God. And if we live this life faithfully, we'll find ourselves sitting by the river in the city of God, basking in the shade of the tree of life as it claps its hands in the light of God! May we help bring as many people into God's eternity as possible!

Apply

If you were built for more than this life then how does that affect how you live day to day? All of life takes different forms. What could God be doing in this form of life to prepare us for what's next?

Do

Share your faith! As surely as the trees grow year to year, God will cause faith to grow in people's hearts if we just keep sharing.

Yield

Lord, help me make the most of this blink of a life between the trees...

Week 11: The Workers Are Few

"The workers are few."

Read
Matthew 9:35-38

The picture painted by Jesus' descriptions of the harvest is a field full of ripe grain or an orchard with trees weighed down by fruit. When a record harvest hangs on the vine, what do we need? We need workers to go into the fields and collect the harvest. We need people to climb up the ladders and get that fruit. So this is a wonderful challenge! The harvest is plentiful. But there is also a sad reality: the workers are few. We are to ask the Lord of the Harvest, since God makes things grow, for more workers.

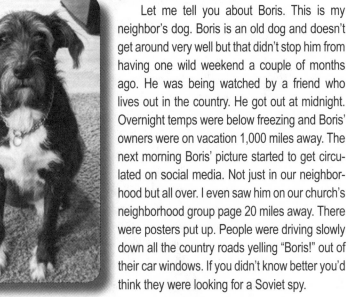

Let me tell you about Boris. This is my neighbor's dog. Boris is an old dog and doesn't get around very well but that didn't stop him from having one wild weekend a couple of months ago. He was being watched by a friend who lives out in the country. He got out at midnight. Overnight temps were below freezing and Boris' owners were on vacation 1,000 miles away. The next morning Boris' picture started to get circulated on social media. Not just in our neighborhood but all over. I even saw him on our church's neighborhood group page 20 miles away. There were posters put up. People were driving slowly down all the country roads yelling "Boris!" out of their car windows. If you didn't know better you'd think they were looking for a Soviet spy.

A woman drove down my driveway and asked if I had seen the dog and I explained that I was already looking every chance I got and that the dog is my neighbor's. She didn't even know she was next to the dog's house. She was just driving down every driveway and asking every person who was outside in the area. This lady explained to me that she was armed with bacon and pork chops in her car and that we should check water sources. Then she slowly drove off yelling Boris out of the window of her car.

Eventually we got word that Boris was found pretty early on and put in the overnight drop off at the local animal shelter. Whew! But then we found out that he somehow escaped from there as well and was on the run again. He was eventually found 10 miles from home with a new gold chain and a tattoo of a chihuahua.

What struck me over that weekend was the instant and incredible effort that went into finding this lost dog. It was all over social media. Lansing, all the suburbs, China for all I know. People dropped everything to drive around with processed meat. People were willing to stop and inconvenience others and talk to strangers in hopes of saving this dog. It was a huge response and the dog was found. I'm not saying it was overboard at all or that because it's a dog, it shouldn't have been such a big deal. Dogs are special members of our families. I think the reaction was totally appropriate.

> **Here's my question though: Why don't we have the same urgency for lost people?**

Here's what I see: Boris was in a place of weakness and vulnerability. Everyone who heard the story knew it: cold temps, a bad hip, an old dog, family out of town. It's a compelling and clear need. There's no way this dog is going to pull an Incredible Journey and find his way home on his own. Boris wasn't going to save himself. He needed someone to rescue him.

For some reason we don't look at people in the same way. Maybe people are better at covering up what's wrong. Dog's don't have the pride to lie about how they're feeling. And I think pride is the real issue. People don't want to seem weak. And I think we kind of expect people to be strong. That makes it even harder. When a person is lost (lost in illness, depression, addiction, sin, toxic relationships—all the ways we get lost) instead of sounding the alarm and jumping in our cars with bacon we have a tendency to cross our arms and shake our heads and wonder why they can't figure out life better. "How are they going to get out of this one?" "I'm glad that's not me!" We have this expectation that people should save themselves when they get into trouble. Maybe we'll help them, if they ask.

This is not how Jesus sees people at all! Why did Jesus go around the towns a preaching and a healing? Because when he saw people he had compassion for them because they were harassed and helpless, sheep without a shepherd. In Jesus' eyes it's like we're all just a bunch of lost dogs! Then he tells his disciples we need more workers in the field. We need to yell out the window, and put up posters, and call all our friends, and put bacon in our cars! There are lost people out there that need to be found!

The harvest is plentiful, the workers are few.

Help Wanted

One of the sad by-products of today's American Christianity, easy-believism, is that it makes "believers" instead of disciples who make more disciples. We don't need more mere believers, Jesus says we need workers! What does it look like to be a worker in God's harvest? What does it look like to be a disciple of Jesus? I've put together a job description.

Clear Spiritual Vision

Pilots have to have 20/20 vision to fly for the Air Force. God's workers need to see through the eyes of the Spirit. We need to see things with God's eyes:

The church in Laodicea stopped having God's vision and look what happened.

Read Revelation 3:15-18.

First of all Jesus is looking at their works. It's not faith vs. works it's a faith that works that counts. God is looking for workers. He saves. We work. The church stopped working and the problem was their eyes. They thought they were prosperous and had no need but in reality they were so needy they couldn't even clothe themselves.

We have to see the reality that the Spirit wants to show us. The scriptures teach that there is "No one righteous—not one." But we see someone with a nice house, job, career, family and we think that because they are rich in this life, they are probably rich in God as well. "No one is righteous" is not an excuse to judge... It's a summons to love. The Spirit wants us to see that people are hurting. People can't save themselves. The most put together person you know still needs Jesus. Can you see it? Can you have compassion like Jesus did? Will you get to work?

Always On Call
Read 2 Timothy 4:1-5

Remember the last chapter? In season and out of season. With the presence

of Jesus who promised to always be with us, it's always harvest time. Being a worker for God isn't a 9 to 5. It's 24/7. When you're taking your orders from the Spirit,
you're always on call.

> I'm not saying that you don't have free time or interests or time
> for your family and yourself. What I'm saying is that everything that
> we do is open to be used by God for the harvest. My kids play sports
> so I can share my faith with the dads. Wherever I live is my field. I
> need to be ready to react to the Spirit's prompt to love someone or
> help someone or beg someone to respond to Jesus in some way.

This is even true in my times with God, I read and pray so I can grow closer
to God, but also so I'll be fully prepared when the Spirit moves in my heart to get
to work.

You've been reading about being hometown missionaries for almost 3 months.
What will be different when you reach the end of this book? It's up to you to make
this a lifestyle and not just a program that you did. Are you ready, in season and out
of season to share life with the lost?

A Thankless Job With A Very Low Wage

Being a worker for God is a thankless job. It has to be.

Read Luke 22:24-30

Jesus showed us with his life and death that working for God doesn't bring
glory in this life. We could recline at the table. We could be the ones who are served
or we could position our lives to be servants. In my life, before I worked in the full-
time ministry and in the full-time ministry, with my friends, with my family, I have
positioned myself as a servant. I love to serve (most of the time).

What position are in you? Are you always the boss? Are you the scheduler?
Are you the critic or the optimizer? Jesus has called us first to be servants who give
God the glory. In the gospel of John, Jesus says it over and over. It's as if he wants
to make sure he doesn't forget it himself. He's not doing anything for his own glory
but for the glory of the Father who sent him.

It's a thankless job. Even eternity with God isn't earned by our work. It's assigned because of his work. We work and we earn nothing and remembering that
keeps us in the low position God desires. There's no Christian corporate ladder. The
dream job is on the lowest rung, being a humble servant that glorifies God!

Get Messy

I don't think I could ever be a nurse. I have so much respect for healthcare workers. My mom is a nurse. It's just too messy for me. There's a lot of poop and pee and blood. Messy! Exhausting!

But being a worker for God, being a missionary in your hometown, can be just as messy and tiring. People's lives get messy. We know this because we can see it in our own lives. Yet we're often shocked when we see someone else's brokenness or shame! Here's what Jesus did when he saw people's messes: He got messy. He entered into their brokenness. He enters into our brokenness:

- A bleeding woman touched him and he stopped what he was doing to hear her story and to tell her it was her faith that healed her.

- A crooked tax collector was moved to see Jesus. Being a short man, Zacchaeus climbed a tree. Jesus went to him and said I'm eating at your house tonight. I'm entering into your life as you repent of your greed.

- A father came begging Jesus to help his son who was demon possessed. Our children show our vulnerabilities like no one else can. And Jesus doesn't just cast out the demon. He talks to the dad, asks questions that he already knew the answer to, and ultimately gets the dad to pray and have faith. He heals the boy, but he saves that dad!

Again and again, the gospels are filled with the most amazing stories of Jesus, the son of God, inserting himself into people's lives and loving the lost until they are found. It shouldn't surprise us that he's promised to be with each one of us through his Spirit and that when we sin he doesn't abandon us as we often imagine in our insecurity. On the contrary, those times of struggle are the very reason why he's there!

Okay, now that you see the requirements are you up for the job? Do you even want the job?

Do you want to see through people's lies and see the world through God's eyes?

Will you be on call in season and out of season? Whatever you do, serving the lost is the reason?

Can you not be in it for the praise but glorifying God as a servant all of your days?

Entering into the brokenness and the mess, if you want this job—say yes!

Here's what you just signed up for, go ahead and read it one more time:

Matthew 9:35-38

Adventure!
   You've signed up for a life of adventure. Uncertainty, impact, healing, helping. It's the most amazing life!

It could read: The harvest is plentiful, but the adventurers are few. Pray earnestly to be sent out as an adventurer for the Lord. Where will God take you without taking you anywhere at all? Whose life will you impact? Who will you lead to the healing power of Christ? How will you be changed by the adventure that is being a laborer for God's kingdom?

We are to pray for more to be sent out. You've been praying every day at the end of the training devotionals. Your church may be organizing a special time of prayer. When you pray, don't just pray for your friends to become Christians. Pray for laborers, workers, servants, adventurers to join you and your church in this hometown mission. Speaking of church, do your part to help every single person in your church to be on the mission. That's so special.

This is what we get to live for as workers in the fields:

We read the parable of the weeds last chapter. Right after explaining that parable, Jesus gives two mini-parables about the kingdom. They give us one last piece of insight into our job as servants who go out and find the lost:

Read Matthew 13:44-46

People can be so proud at times that it may even seem offensive to regard them as "lost". Who are we to declare that, anyway? But it's not so much that someone is missing, it's what they're missing out on that can motivate us without turning us into judgmental jerks. If you are a part of the kingdom of God, then you've got this treasure and this map (gospel! Bible!) that you can share. If you aren't active in the kingdom of God—loving people, getting deep, being dependable and vulnerable—then you might just be missing out yourself.

God gets people ready so that when they see the kingdom, like a person who stumbles across a treasure in a field, they will sell all they have, give up what they were treasuring to get the real treasure.

Are people stumbling across the kingdom when they meet you? When they see the way you follow God, the way you joyfully embark on adventure, do they realize that this is what they've been searching for all along?

We have the treasure. We hold the pearl of great price. Unless we're burying our treasure or hiding the gift of God, or forgetting that we were all Boris. We were just as helpless; shivering in the night, covered in briars and searching for home. And God found us. God brought us home. Imagine the joy Boris had when he made it home. Think about how that tail must have uncontrollably wagged and the joy my neighbors children had to have their lost friend back from the brink. This is the joy we offer as we share our faith with the lost. Our friends get to find God and be found by him!

This is Boris after being found and reunited with his family.
It's time to get to work!

Week 11: In the Field Training

I wonder how often we miss out on spiritual adventures because we don't know what we're supposed to be doing. Whenever my kids say that they're bored I say, "Find something to do." Are we bored in God's kingdom? Would it help if we knew what to do? This week, as we come close to the end of our hometown missionary training, we'll look at six spiritual occupations. May these "God jobs" be what occupies each of us. Until the day that all are saved or Jesus comes back, there's no room for boredom in the church and in the world. The harvest is plentiful, the workers are few! We can be the answer to the apostles' prayers for more workers by getting to work as hometown missionaries!

As you read about these 6 biblical occupations, think about which job would be the best fit for your life. **God calls us all to the mission, but he uses each of us in ways that are unique to us as individuals.** May you discover your calling as a missionary through the word of God this week. Share about your new job #HometownMissionary #GodJobs #TheWorkersAreFew on social media this week. Before you start this week's devotionals, fill out this application that you'll refer back to at the end of the week.

Kingdom Job Application
Fill this out with your family for this week's family devotional activity

Name _____

Special Skills (What are you good at?) _____

Interests (Things you love) _____

How could God use those things for his greater work?_____

Circle all that apply to you below. Look back at this as you go through this week's lessons. **I enjoy or I am good at:**

Caring for people Listening Working through problems Giving credit to others

Sharing the gospel with strangers "Me Time" Discovering new hobbies

My work or career Giving more than getting Volunteering Making good money

Having inspiring or challenging talks Speaking the truth in love Working hard

Having Scriptures to share Keeping busy Valuing details Understanding my role

Staying focused amid distractions Following directions Keeping priorities in check

*How's your Mission Map looking? Take a moment to fill in the places and people you've shared with!

Monday: Help Wanted—Be a Soldier _____

Read
2 Timothy 2:1-13
2 Timothy 4:6-8

Examine
In these passages and a few others the connection is made between serving Christ and being a soldier. Obviously this analogy is limited since we would never physically fight for the kingdom but the spiritual battle we engage in shares many similarities with the theater of war. We've already seen in Ephesians 6 that we are fighting the dark forces of evil in our world and never other people, who are our mission, not our enemies. In this passage we get advice on how to be more effective in the fight for the souls of men and women.

First of all, a good soldier does not get involved in civilian affairs. The job is to please the commanding officer; to follow orders to the best of our ability. Getting distracted by "civilian pursuits" still makes the headlines in our world today when officers get in trouble for things that they tried to keep private. Paul urges Timothy to not allow himself to be entangled but to stay focused on the mission.

How often are we taken out of the noble fight because of "civilian pursuits"? The urgent but unimportant can steal our focus from what truly matters. A soldier must rise above the noise and fulfill the duty to which she has been assigned. We must "go and make disciples" regardless of what is going on around us. The busyness of life is actually the perfect place to fulfill our commission if we don't get distracted!

Apply
What civilian pursuits have been entangling you? They may need to be cut out

of your life but it also may be possible to just approach the mundane with a new perspective. How can you turn the mundane into mission?

Do

Share your faith today while you live your life. Bring your mission into the shopping line, carpool or whatever other civilian activities you regularly engage in. You are living in your mission field.

Yield

Lord, help me to always be in the fight no matter what life throws at me...

Tuesday: Help Wanted—Be a Farmer _____

Read

2 Timothy 2:6-7
1 Corinthians 3:6-9
Matthew 20:1-16

Examine

Our jobs are often a source of pride or discouragement. It is hard to separate what we do from who we are. In many of Jesus' parables we are described as farm workers. Not the owner of the farm but merely the hired hand that helps with the landowner's harvest. This is a humble position! We can't really take pride in being a farmhand but instead we can take pride in our Lord who sees us as special and has called us to work his field.

The parable of the laborers in the vineyard highlights our humble position and God's greatness in a memorable way. We are the workers hired in the last hour. The people of Israel and all the Christ followers who came before us labored for God, laying a foundation for our lives as Christians today. Think about how good we have it. The Hebrews could only look forward and wonder about how God would save. Their hopes are our promises. And yet we can expect the same gracious reward from the Father.

Knowing that we are working close to the sunset and not in the heat of the day should fill us with joy and gratitude as we work on the mission field all around us. How many who call themselves Christians are still standing idle in the marketplace wondering how they can serve God? Hopefully these devotionals have been a clear call to get to work. The good news is, no matter how long you've been standing idle,

God wants to bless you with the same grace he's always shown to those who are his. In the end, it's not about our performance but his generosity. Let's get into the fields before the sun sets!

Apply

Are you still wondering how to get to work for God? Your field is all around you—start recruiting more workers. God makes it grow—all you can do is work by praying and sharing your faith. You may not bring in a huge harvest yourself but maybe you'll meet someone who becomes an evangelist, church planter or foreign missionary.

Do

Let the thought of God's grace in your life overflow as you share your faith today. Remember you are planting a seed just as people have done for the last 2,000 years. Those seeds resulted in your salvation!

Yield

God, I praise you for your undeserved grace, help me to sow your grace in this field where you've planted me...

Wednesday: Help Wanted—Be a Potter _____

Read
Jeremiah 18:1-10
Jeremiah 19:1-2, 10-11
Romans 9:19-26

God sends Jeremiah on some amazing field trips! First, he goes to visit a potter and watch him work the wheel. As the clay is built up and then smashed in the potter's hands, God proclaims to Jeremiah that his people are the clay. He is totally in control of the rise and fall of nations and individuals. Next, Jeremiah takes the leaders of Israel with him to the valley of Ben Hinnom, the trash dump of Jerusalem. Today, landfills are filled with plastic bags. Their dumps were full of broken pottery. Jeremiah smashes a dried-out pot and proclaims God's judgment against Israel. In a complicated section of Romans, Paul speaks of God's choice to make Christ's followers into the new Israel by using the metaphor of a potter with clay. Wouldn't we be shocked if a sandwich we made started talking back to us and telling us that we made it wrong? In the same way, God is totally in control of his creation. Thankfully, he loves us as his people instead of devouring us like a sandwich! And he even listens to us!

In these texts we are the clay and God is the potter who is constantly molding his people. There is, however, one aspect of the potter's job that we can and should do. We can't mold people. I will repeat that: we have no control over molding or changing people. That's God's job! But we can help people stay soft and moldable. There's a big difference between Jeremiah 18 and 19. The clay at the potter's house is wet and can be molded. Surely it must have been painful to see it smashed in the potter's hands but as long as the clay stays moldable it can be rebuilt into whatever purpose God has for it. The clay at the valley of Ben Hinnom is another story. It has become brittle and cracked and can only be thrown away. There is no recovery for a heart that has become this hard. In fact, the valley of Ben Hinnom is a root for the New Testament word used for hell, "gehenna". Jesus' description of a place where the worm does not die and the fire is not quenched is a description of the same trash valley that Jeremiah visited.

Sharing our faith isn't always an invitation to church or a Bible study. A lot of times when we share our faith it doesn't result in the immediate salvation of our friend. Many times mentioning Jesus or the love of God simply serves the purpose of softening someone's heart, of keeping them from the point of no return that ends with a hard heart in hell. In this way we partner with the potter and stand with the Spirit as he readies people's hearts to be built up for salvation.

Apply

How can your prayers and words help keep people's hearts soft toward God? If we aren't careful/tactful with how we share our faith do you see how we can sometimes harden people's hearts? Examine your own heart. Are there ways that you have become hardened? How can you become more moldable again?

Do

Share your faith today in a way that could make someone more inclined to hear the gospel in the future. Talk about God or your faith like it's just a regular part of your life. God can use you to help mold souls for salvation!

Yield

Lord, mold me into whatever I need to be to advance your kingdom and your will...

Thursday: Help Wanted—Be a Tentmaker _____

Read
Acts 18:1-4
2 Corinthians 11:1-11
Colossians 3:23-24

Examine

Isn't it amazing to think that the greatest missionary in history, the apostle Paul, worked a skilled trade job as he did his ministry? While he did accept support in some places and did not oppose ministry workers being paid for their work, he often chose to labor for the gospel while working as a tentmaker. Aquila and Priscilla became fast friends because they shared the same occupation and probably the same workspace. Can you imagine buying a goat hair tent made by the apostle Paul? That would be quite the collector's item!

Being a "tentmaker" has become analogous to working in the ministry without pay. We should be so grateful to those who lead churches and ministries while being self-supported. But we should also strive to see ourselves as tent-makers who work our skilled trades or careers so we ourselves can be self-supported hometown missionaries. If Paul did it, you can as well! While you're at work, you're on the mission. Part of the reason you have the job you have is that your co-workers need to hear about Jesus. And when you aren't at work you get to be on the mission: spending time with God, loving your family and serving the lost and the church. That's the tentmaker life!

There's a temptation to work more than we have to or to climb the success ladder. We falsely believe that it will get easier after we get to the next rung. We don't have to fall for these work life traps if we have God's perspective on our jobs. Like everything else in this world, our jobs are an opportunity to glorify God. Whatever we do, we can do it with joy as we work hard because we have a bigger boss: God! And as we produce for our companies/employers, we can have the satisfaction of knowing that we are also producing fruit for God as we work. It's all about the perspective we bring. Our work doesn't keep us from being close to God or from having an impact. It's the very tool God wants to use to complete the mission in your hometown.

Apply

How can your workplace be more of a mission field? What could you do before work to remind yourself that you're really punching in on God's clock and serving him? How will a tentmaker's heart help you glorify God even more when you aren't working?

Do

Share your faith at work today and praise God for giving you a mission field that pays the bills!

Yield

Lord, help all of my work to be for you...

Friday: Help Wanted—Be a Fisherman _____

Read
Matthew 4:12-22
John 21:1-17

Examine

Jesus chose fishermen as his first disciples. This well known fact isn't news to us but it would have been a great surprise to Israel. Historically, the people of Israel were shepherds and farmers all the way back to Cain and Abel. Think of how many fishermen we are told about in the Old Testament? Does Jonah count? There are none. The Sea of Galilee (Sea of Kinneret) is scarcely even mentioned in the Old Testament. And yet that's where Jesus goes fishing for disciples fulfilling Isaiah's prophecy that a light would dawn on Galilee of the Gentiles.

Jesus famously calls them to drop their nets but promises to give them a new purpose as "fishers of men". The fact that these first disciples were fishermen tells us a couple of things. First, they did not have the chops to be disciples of a rabbi. They failed out of college prep and had to take on a skilled trade. And second, they came from a long line of fishermen. Thus, when Jesus calls them he is not looking for the brightest and the best, but merely the willing. And these first disciples certainly proved their willingness. To respond to the call of Christ they gave up more than a job. They were willing to abandon their purposes (being fishermen and raising fishermen just as their ancestors had) to take up this new purpose. Fishing was completely transformed by Jesus' call.

Jesus calls us in the same way. He doesn't want you to abandon who you are to follow him. He wants you to bring all of your skill and experience and allow him to transform it into something he can use for a greater purpose than you could have ever imagined. Your career, your hobbies and interests, your talents and desires, were given to you by God so you could be the amazing person that you are. If you let God take hold of those things and use them for the hometown mission, then everything you do will have a greater purpose. All the parts of our lives are redeemed when we give them to God. Peter exemplifies this. He started as a fisherman and Jesus trained him to become a fisher of men but in the end there was an even greater purpose that Peter needed to surrender to. He would no longer fish but shepherd. In many ways this shift back to the traditional occupation of Israel shows us the power of God to make our lives into something so much greater when we give everything (jobs, hobbies, relationships) into his all powerful, all knowing and all loving hands.

Apply
What interests and skills make you who you are? How could God use your strengths and desires to do amazing things for his purposes? Often we feel guilty about working so much or doing "me time" activities. How could you let God use those things so you don't have to lose those things?

Do
Share your faith while doing something that you love! Pray for God to cast a wide net with your life, pulling fish from all the areas of activity you engage in.

Yield
Lord, use the things that I love to do to make a greater impact than I could ever imagine...

Saturday: Help Wanted—Be a Shepherd _____

Read
1 Peter 5:1-5
Titus 1:5-9

Examine
As we saw yesterday, as Jesus reinstated Peter, he changed his calling from that of a fisher of men to a shepherd of sheep. Of all the occupations we've looked at this week, shepherd (elder) is the only actual position that we find in the church. Why did Peter need to shift from fishing to shepherding? Besides fulfilling the

destiny of Israel as a nation of shepherds, when we compare these jobs there is one important difference. A shepherd knows his sheep. Both jobs are messy but shepherding is personal. Sheep aren't that bright. They never figure out how to survive on their own. Yet they are loved and cared for. Shepherding describes the way God relates to us and it makes so much sense that post-denial Peter would never fish again as he learned to become a shepherd.

Late in his life we read his words to other shepherds and we can be so inspired by his transformation. This small town family fisherman had indeed been transformed by God into a shepherd. And just as Jesus encouraged Peter to feed his sheep before he went to heaven, Peter is encouraging others to take up the job of shepherding at the end of his life. His instruction makes it clear that shepherding in the church is more than a job. It's a calling to lead joyfully and and eagerly by example and to do it to please God and not ourselves.

In Titus (and 1 Timothy 3) we are given the qualifications of eldership (shepherds). These lists are useful for all who desire to work for the souls of men and women who are already in the church and those who will be someday. God needs shepherds and his word tells us what the life of a spiritual shepherd is like. My greatest desire is to be counted as an elder/shepherd someday. I praise God that I can check my growth and progress against passages like these as I strive to do my best work for his kingdom and his people. Let's all strive to be shepherds even as we await the return of the Chief Shepherd and overseer of our souls!

Apply

If you applied to be an elder/overseer/shepherd would you get the job? When you look at the qualifications of eldership what do you need to work on that is in your control? How can you apply the role of shepherd to your life regardless of your title or leadership position?

Do

Share your faith with the loving heart of a shepherd. It might get messy but that's part of the job! Jump into the mess with the Spirit as your guide as you lovingly pull your friend closer to the Good Shepherd.

Yield

"Lord, help my church to be full of caring shepherds...

Bonus:

Job Placement:
Which job is best for you? Look back at the skills you circled at the beginning of the week. Each line is associated with a kingdom occupation from top to bottom: Shepherd, Fisherman, Tentmaker, Potter, Farmer, Soldier. Which lines had the most circles? How could knowing your spiritual occupation help you as a hometown missionary? How could you grow in other areas in order to do even more for God?

*Go back over this with your family before next week's family devotional

Week 12: The Celebration of the Saints

"And they began to celebrate."

—Luke 12:24

We started with the heart of God and we'll end there too. Seeing God in a new way, in the Jesus way, is true repentance. God's heart is that all people would repent and see things his way. So when Jesus spoke he tried again and again to show people what his Father was really like. In Luke chapter 15 Jesus has a conversation with the religious leaders of his day in which he strives to rewrite their image of God by telling the same story three times and then throwing a gut punch in at the end. This is my favorite chapter in the whole Bible.

Set the stage for the heart of God by reading Luke 15:1-3.

There are 3 groups converging in this moment. You've got Jesus and his disciples. Then there are the tax collectors and sinners, which is a way of saying the non-practicing Jewish people. And last, you've got the Pharisees and scribes who are grumbling about Jesus welcoming sinful people into his life and teaching. In response to this grumbling Jesus tells three parables. Three is an important Bible number. It's the number of the trinity. It means Jesus is going to show us what God is really like. Do you want to know what God is really like?

Well here's how Jesus describes his Father in Luke 15:4-24.

God is jealous for you, he's stalking you on Facebook right now. He doesn't know when to quit. The God of the Bible is the kind of lover that you get a restraining order on. He's broken hearted and he might do something that sounds crazy.

In fact as the Old Testament closes and the New begins, he does do something crazy. He does something completely over the top, something embarrassing and undignified. Have you ever loved someone so much that you can't help but act funny around that person and later on you look back and wonder what you were thinking? Well God, the creator of the universe, the all powerful, all knowing being that gives us life and creates black holes and understands sub-atomic particles does this wild thing: He decides to become one of us.

It's a wild, love imbibed decision (but it had always been the plan). It's this over the top effort to get us to notice him again. And so when we get to the New Testament we read about Jesus, a man who has inside of him all the passion and love and jealousy and desire that God has. Imagine a man with a heart like that?

Jesus shows us with his life and death and tells us in these parables that God doesn't *kind of* love you. He doesn't passively love you. He is not nonchalant, un-caring, uninvolved even if that's what you think.

This is who God is: God is a shepherd and you are his sheep. And if you are not with him, he will run through the fields and he will search in every marsh and bush until he finds you scared, alone, bleating and bleeding. And when he finds you, he will not punish you or scold you or eat you for dinner. He will joyfully put you and all of your mess on his shoulders and run you back to where you belong with the biggest smile on his face. He'll tell his friends about you. He'll brag about how awesome you are and throw a party. Not because you did anything, but just because you were found.

> **Such is the obsessive love of God.**

This is who God is: God is a woman looking for a coin that she lost. She can't think of anything but this coin. She wants it so bad. She tears the house apart (you know like when you lose your keys or even worse, the remote) and she looks under the furniture and she checks every possible place and retraces her steps. Nothing matters except finding that coin. And when she finds it, when he finds you, he calls the neighborhood together and throws a party! Who throws a party when they find a lost coin? Someone who is crazy.

> **Such is the crazy love of God.**

This is who God is: God is a father. Hurt by his foolish son, he could be filled with bitterness. But instead, every night before the sun sets he goes out to scan the horizon, just hoping that his son's silhouette will appear. And when his son finally returns he does not lecture or say "I told you so". He doesn't even let him apologize. He runs for him. Imagine this old man pulling up his robe and sprinting down the lane in his bare feet. Imagine him engulfing his son in this monster hug and kissing him and yelling to his servants, "Fire up the barbecue! My son, my love, the only thing I've ever wanted is back! Let's have a party!"

Such is the inexplicable love of God.

How did we get this idea that God is just waiting for the moment that we mess up so he can strike us with lightning? The truth is he is waiting for the moment he can party with us!

And they began to celebrate!

Now remember who Jesus is talking to. He's talking to the religious people of his day. And you have to think that even the most hard hearted and prideful Pharisee in the group was amazed at Jesus' description of God. Aren't you so encouraged that our God will not rest until he finds what is lost and that when the lost are found there's a party that shakes the heavens and the earth! Amazing! He won't stop looking for the people we're reaching out to! You're reading this book (and more importantly, his book) because he refused to stop looking for you!

Now if you have some religiosity in you as you read this. You know, the kind of person that is judgmental and critical and holier than thou and forgets that you were lost and a lot of times still get lost, then you just want the story to end where we stopped reading. You want to be done with the hometown missionary book! Just close it now if you want. Everyone goes home feeling good. God is so loving. Angel parties! Awesome. But there's one more paragraph and for the religious people (us!) that's so painful. Are you still reading? Are you ready?

O Brother!
Read it in Luke 15:25-32

Where's the older son? In the field. He's working for the father. We've talked about the harvest and being out in the mission field a lot over the last 12 weeks. I hope you engaged with the training and the challenges and that you started to see how God can work through every disciple including you! I hope that you didn't look around and try to judge how engaged other people in your church or small group were. I'm grateful our church isn't like that, but we all have our moments.

The older brother comes near to the house and he hears music and dancing. He's been out there working. He's been serving and giving and being righteous and there's a celebration going on?! Interestingly he doesn't go right to his Father.

Maybe there's some distance there. He asks a servant what's going on and gets the news. His little brother has come home. The one who took the inheritance, turned his back on the family, wished dad would just die so he could take his money.

We know the father's heart had always been love and compassion and longing for his son.

But what about the older brother's heart all those years? I think he wanted punishment, revenge, judgment. And isn't that how so many people see God? They think God is like this older brother waiting to punish us for our sin. We struggle not to see God like this ourselves sometimes. Have you ever wondered why people think God is angry and vengeful instead of seeing how much he loves us and how he's waiting with open arms to receive us even when we abandon him? I wonder if it's because people can't see the Father, but they sure do see a lot of older brothers sitting in church every Sunday. May that never be the case where you sit! But we have to guard our hearts! When you get out there working in the field, it's so easy to look over your shoulder and start to judge.

I mean, look at his reasoning. I've put in the years. Where's my party? If you've been a Christian for a while, surely you've felt like this at some point. I've been following Jesus all these years, why is life still so difficult?

We feel joy when someone gets baptized but maybe a little skepticism as well? "Oh, you just wait till you dry off and Satan gets to work on you." I know I'm going to some dark places in this celebration chapter but the reason Jesus told these three stories about the heart of God was to get to this last story about the hearts of the religious. So we must go there too.

It does seem a little unfair that the fattened calf got killed for this newbie. I mean what about us? The older son actually confronts the father and I'm so glad he does because we get the answer from the father. We get to see why God is so quick to celebrate when a lost sheep or coin or son or you or me gets found in those first three stories and in the months to come as you work as a hometown missionary. Here's what God thinks about those who've been faithful over the years; listen to God's tender-hearted love for you older brother, older sister:

> *"Son, daughter, you are always with me, and all that is mine is yours."*

What did you need? What were you upset about or critical about? Who were you comparing your righteousness to? Doesn't that squelch all of our religious pride?

So we don't want to be like the older brother but we do want to be working in the fields as hometown missionaries. The book has come to an end, the training devotionals are done. How can we stay active and be righteous but avoid becoming religious? We actually read the answer to this question at the very beginning of the chapter. The first three verses of Luke 15 show us that we simply need to strive to have the same reputation that Jesus had.

Listen to this: You've got Jesus, you've got a real relationship with the Father who's crazy about you, you're out there in the field working for the kingdom as you go about your life. All of that is great, but it comes with the older brother warning: Caution—your mission may become religious pride unless people can say this about you:

"This person receives sinners and eats with them."

That's the heart of God. That's the task of a hometown missionary. And when we have a reputation for showing hospitality and love to those who need God you better believe God is going to give us so much to celebrate.

Check out your Mission Map. Think about what it looked like on day one. It always looks like that if your minister is the only missionary in your hometown. Now look at your map and imagine everyone in your church with a map filled with Mission Moments. Think about the impact in your hometown in just three months! That's something to celebrate! And we're not celebrating what we did or the stars we scribbled on a map. We're celebrating God and his plan to use us when we obey him.

The Father says this to each of us: "I am always with you and all that I have is yours." And then we share our faith and see his power working through us and all over our communities and you know that it's true. It's not just a story about a family with a father and two brothers. It's the story of God's family right here in your hometown and it's still being written! So what can we do to continue as Hometown Missionaries even as your training comes to an end?

The secret to being a grateful servant and not becoming a critical Christian is so simple. It's probably one of the first lessons we learned as children but maybe something that some kids never learn. And if you remember nothing else about being a hometown missionary, remember this:

Share

All that God has is yours, so share.

The Pharisees, the older brothers, the religious, they want God all to themselves as if they'll run out. Their idea of God is so small that they want to keep him for themselves. They want to keep the "sinners" away so God won't get ruined, as if we could ruin a perfect and all powerful God!

We're not going to run out of fattened calf! There's no shortage of rings or robes.

We're not going to run out of faith—so let's keep sharing it.

We're not going to run out of food or shelter—so let's share it.

We're not going to run out of joy—so let's share it!

Your father wants you to know that you are always with him and that he has shared everything with you! It's not about what you have, or your performance, or what you know, or how you feel, it's all about what he has given you and that he is with you.

That's something we can all celebrate! That's something we can all share. We don't need to hang around outside the party sulking. It's time to sing and dance with the angels for everyone who was lost and now is found, for everyone who was dead but is now alive.

We have so much to celebrate! Things get hard for all of us at times. I see a lot as a church leader because I'm involved with a lot of the tough stuff and the sin that creeps in or that we jump in. But I still celebrate. I still have so much joy.

Did you know that we are referred to as "Saints" almost 100 times in the Bible? Yeah you! A saint! That means that God sees you that way. He knows you've run off and got dirty and you got lost between the couch cushions and you got into the pig food and some wild living but you came back. You got found. And your father sees you as perfect! A saint! How about that!

That's why there's just so much to celebrate even in hard times. I see people who were addicted. I see people whose marriages were on the rocks. I've seen what God can do to a family, how God can change a man, how faithful you can be through really hard times, and I rejoice. I celebrate with the saints!

I don't know exactly what's going to happen with all the people you've met in the last 12 weeks. But I hope you're ready to work with them and to stay on the mission; to share, share, share! Because God wants to celebrate. The angels are tuning their instruments and putting cookies and tacos out. There's a bunch of little brothers and sisters out there who need to come back to God and experience the family that is your church and his kingdom, the saints of your hometown. Now that's something to celebrate.

No training devotionals for this last week, just a thoughtful guide to help you pinpoint what God wants you to learn from this book and this experience. If you've made an effort as a Hometown Missionary then you have so much to celebrate! Even when the prodigal son returned, it was only the beginning of the celebration. Our lives in Christ are Jubilee until Christ returns to bring us into the great wedding banquet. Hope tells us that the celebration of God will never end! Celebrate as you think of all the ways God has worked in your life these last three months.

Do

Pray through this after you finish filling it out it and you could have one of the best praise sessions of your life! Talk through these questions with your family and celebrate all that God has done together.

Make sure you fill out the Mission Map at church with all of your personal missionary activity if your church is doing this book together

What is something that you learned about God from the chapters, training devotionals or challenges?

What is something you learned about yourself as a follower of Jesus on the mission?

What does "gospel" mean to you?

What new insights do you have about Jesus?

What is the boldest thing you've done in the last 12 weeks?

How did you show hospitality? What impact was had? How will you continue to be hospitable?

What were the most positive responses you had when you shared your faith? Did you have a Bible study or a friend at church or a good conversation?

Where there any negative responses or missed opportunities to share your faith?

Did you attend a Bible talk, gospel night or special event related to this book? What did the Spirit show you at those events?

Who will you continue to pray for and reach out to on your mission field?

Did you learn how to be a missionary in your hometown? Is there anything else you wish you could learn?

Important: *God makes things grow!* Being a Hometown Missionary is not about your performance but his grace. So praise God for the journey he has you on and dream with him about the ways he could use you to impact your town for his glory in the future!

Share your story at www.hometownmissionary.com by filling out an anonymous survey.

Epilogue
You've Become A Hometown Missionary. What Will God Do?

There was a woman in Lansing who worked midnights in the NICU at the hospital. This might be the most isolated place in Lansing. It's on lockdown. She was searching for God and God was searching for her. But with her extreme schedule and isolated work environment how would she ever be reached out to?

Well, God let my wife and I have a sick baby so we could go up there and meet her. I really believe that's the only way someone could have met her. We were there in the NICU every day for almost 2 months with Emelia. In that time nurse Jodi comforted us when we were low and we shared the gospel with her and invited her to church. A couple of months later she was baptized. She's the most amazing nurse and she's your sister in Christ. A few months later her 70-year-old mom got baptized. Then a year later two of her friends got baptized. And on top of all of that our daughter is now 6 years old and perfectly healthy.

What a humbling picture of the power of God's grace. When God needs someone (or four someones) saved, he's powerful enough to accomplish his task with even a sick baby as his missionary! Who's waiting to hear the gospel of grace from you and how will God accomplish his will? You are a hometown missionary and every corner of your life is your mission field. May God use you in the most amazing ways as a missionary in your hometown!

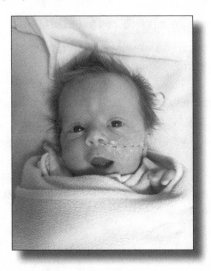

Appendix A

Old School Bible Study Series
Introduction and Methodology

Old School

Jesus' plan was for all of his disciples to be able to go and make disciples, even if they never went beyond their hometowns. As a church leader, my desire is to have a church full of disciples who can make disciples. In order to do this I expect myself to provide the training and resources that will help each Christian to be a Christian on the mission.

To accomplish this, we print Bible study outlines for people to give to their friends. We've gone through many versions. You can check them out at KingdomBuiltResources.com. All of our resources are available in high quality format through amazon for the lowest possible price.

Currently, most of the people in our church are using Old School as a guide for studying the Bible with their friends. The study series doesn't matter. It's the gospel that it points to that has the power of salvation. I have found that having a resource like Old School helps inspire confidence and is a great jumping off point, especially for less experienced disciple makers.

Methodology

What makes Old School and our other Bible studies unique and effective is their format. They are set up like a workbook. The idea (that works!) is that you give the booklet to your friend and they look at the Scriptures before you meet up. Then when you meet for your Bible study you discuss what they've studied. Anyone can do it! (Even you!)

There are only 5 studies because it was just taking too long to help people make Jesus Lord. We had added a lot of things that could be taught after our friends were added to the church. Of course, you can always break up the studies into smaller chunks as needed or pull an all nighter and baptize someone the next morning!

There is an added benefit to handing out the Bible studies in a workbook format. When your friend finishes the Bible studies he or she has a copy of the studies with all of their notes so they can go and study the Bible with someone else right away.

You don't really need a class to teach these studies but if you want to see our presentation of the Bible studies check out HometownMissionary.com. Lastly, we're always looking for more effective ways to have a church full of disciple makers so these studies are always evolving. And since we won't ever reach perfection this side of eternity that's a good thing. Please feel free to copy and distribute the Old School study series or order in bulk from Amazon via **KingdomBuiltResources.com**.

Old School

Old School by Joel Nagel
For more information and resources check out
lansingchurch.org and
kingdombuiltresources.com

Go Old School In Your Walk With God

"Thus says the Lord: 'Stand by the roads and look,
and ask for the ancient paths, where the good way is; and walk in it and find rest for your
souls.' But they said, 'We will not walk in it.'"
—Jeremiah 6:16

Caution: These five Bible studies will challenge you to your core and you'll never look at
Christianity the same way again—but only if you are open to seeing God's word through
Old School eyes. As a restoration church and ministry, we desire to restore Christianity
to the way it was in the Bible by living as authentic followers of Jesus and not followers
of religious tradition.

Where Do You Stand?   227
    Start Here: A Radical Self-Assessment

Authentic Discipleship   229
    Retro Christianity in a World of Relativism

Authentic Salvation   231
    Immersion in the Original Promise of Salvation

Authentic Community   233
    Deep Commitment in a Shallow Society

Counting the Cost   235
    Going All In and All Out for the All In All

Where Do You Stand?

Start Here: A Radical Self-Assessment

"For the gate is narrow and the way is hard that leads to life, and those who find it are few." —Matthew 7:14

To get where you want to go with God, you have to know where you are starting. Our pride wants us to judge ourselves as better or worse than we are. We want to look good before others when it's only God's opinion that matters. And guess what? He's head over heels in love with you! So, this first Bible study isn't about looking good or bad—it's about being honest—painfully and joyfully real about where you stand in your walk with God. This is for you to do on your own first (if possible) and then to share with a study partner that you trust. You got this!

My Spiritual Timeline

Begin by listing major spiritual events in your life in the space below. (For example: church membership, baptism, major challenges and major changes)

A Letter to a Friend in Need of Salvation

In the space below, write a letter to a real or hypothetical friend detailing how they could become saved. Use scriptures if possible.

Dear _____,

_____

_____

_____

_____

_____

_____

_____

■ List any questions you may have about what the Bible says about salvation:

Strengths and Weaknesses

When you think about your relationship with God, what strengths do you see? In what ways would you like to grow or improve?

Priorities and Commitment

■   List the relationships and responsibilities that are most important to you:

■   What does commitment to God and church mean to you? Describe your idea of being a part of a Christian community:

Spiritual Growth

■   What do you hope to learn from studying the Bible?

The Two Roads

Read the following passages and reflect on your relationship with God. Write down any questions or thoughts that you may want to discuss with your Bible study partner.

Matthew 7:13-14
Matthew 6:33
Luke 13:22-27
Luke 15:1-24

In each of these passages, Jesus is speaking about our hearts and God's heart. How do the words of Jesus make you feel? How might you respond? Take a moment to write down your thoughts:

_____

_____

_____

Next Meet Up with Study Partner _____

Authentic Discipleship
Retro Christianity in a World of Relativism

"Jesus Christ is the same yesterday and today and forever."
—Hebrews 13:8

Here's some good news about the good news: We don't need to invent new ways to follow Jesus. God and his word never need to change. (Because you can't improve on perfection!) So, if we want to be followers of Jesus we just need to look at what Jesus said about following him in the Bible. May it build your faith to see that even as everything in the world seems to always be changing, the ancient truths of following Jesus remain the same.

The Word of God
Read the following passages and take some notes on what the Bible says about itself:

Hebrews 4:12-13

2 Timothy 3:16-17

1 Timothy 4:16

John 8:30-32

The Life of a Christ Follower
Disciples are those who abide in His word. In the following passages, Jesus himself tells us what it looks like to follow him:

Mark 1:14-20

Matthew 28:18-20

Luke 9:23-26

Luke 14:25-33

John 13:34-35

Questions to Explore

■ How important is it to study the Bible?

■ Are you committed to living by the Bible or do you try to make the Bible fit your life?

■ Do you want to be a biblical follower of Christ?

■ What will your life be like as a disciple?

■ What will be challenging? What will be better?

Next Meet Up with Study Partner _____

Notes:

_____

_____

_____

_____

_____

_____

_____

_____

_____

_____

Authentic Salvation
Immersion in the Original Plan of Salvation

"Repent and be baptized every one of you in the name of Jesus Christ
for the forgiveness of your sins, and you will receive the gift of the Holy Spirit."

—Acts 2:38

With all the different ways that God's plan of salvation is presented in churches today, we might start to think that the Bible is unclear or that God left it up to us to figure out how to receive the gift of salvation. If we look to the scriptures, however, there is no grey area. God would never leave us guessing about how we can receive the salvation that his son died to secure! Unfortunately, many have ignored the Bible's clear teaching and adopted practices not found in scripture. May you see once and for all what the Bible says about how we receive forgiveness of sin, the Holy Spirit, and life eternal.

The Problem Is Sin
Before we can talk about salvation we need to look at the only thing keeping us from God: our sin.
Romans 3:23, 6:23
Isaiah 59:1-2
Galatians 5:19-21
James 4:17

God's Response to Our Sin: The Cross
We pushed God out of our lives with sin but he responded with the cross so our relationship with him could be restored. Without his saving action on our behalf we could never be saved.
Isaiah 52:13-53:12, Psalm 22
Matthew 26-28
Romans 5:6-8
2 Corinthians 5:14-21
*This is a good stopping point if running out of time

Our Response: Repentance and Baptism
Even though we could never earn such a priceless gift as salvation, we are still required to take action in order to become saved (have our sins forgiven):
Luke 13:1-5
2 Corinthians 7:10-11
Acts 3:19-21
Acts 2:36-41

Romans 6:1-5
1 Peter 3:18-21
Mark 16:16

Questions to Explore

■ What sins have separated you from God in the past? What sins are you currently struggling with? (James 5:16 on the power of confession)

■ What action did God take in order to provide forgiveness for your sins? How does this make you feel?

■ What are the things that the Bible calls us to do in order to receive salvation?

■ What other ways have you heard or responded to messages of salvation that are not found in the Bible?

■ Why is the original message of salvation presented by Peter in Acts 2 so important to authentic discipleship?

■ How does belief, repentance and baptism connect us to the saving power of the cross?

■ Why is it essential that we die to sin (repent) *before* we get baptized?

■ Have you been saved the way that Luke (Acts), Peter, Paul, the ancient Roman church, and Jesus taught salvation?

■ God has completed his saving work through Jesus on the cross and in the resurrection. What do you need to do to have your sins forgiven, receive the Holy Spirit and be added to the church?

Next Meet Up with Study Partner _____
Notes:

_____

_____

_____

_____

_____

_____

_____

_____

_____

Authentic Community
Deep Commitment in a Shallow Society

"And they devoted themselves to the apostles' teaching and fellowship,
to the breaking of bread and the prayers."

—Acts 2:42

Radical individualism and self-sufficiency are badges of honor in our society, while needing people is often seen as weakness. When these attitudes seep into Christianity, the church becomes a spectator sport with Christians cheering in the stands instead of fighting side by side in the arena. These American ideals would have been foreign ideas to our first century brothers and sisters. In their eyes, even something as personal as salvation was only experienced in community. A meaningful relationship with God can only be experienced when we have meaningful relationships with one another in Christ.

Life Together
Salvation is not an ending but a beginning of our new lives with God and God's people, his church.

Matthew 28:18-20   **Acts 2:42-47**   **Hebrews 10:23-25**

■   What will you do to experience authentic community and be devoted to the church?
■   What priority will church take in your life?

Discipleship
Jesus didn't just teach about discipleship. He modeled it by choosing and sending out his followers in small groups.

Luke 10:1-9   **Matthew 26:36-46**   **Hebrews 3:12-14**

■   How do Jesus and his disciples practice discipleship in these passages? How can you imitate?
■   Every member of our church participates in discipleship groups. Talk with your study partner about how to begin experiencing life in Christian community.

Body Building
Check out these passages that describe the church as an organism, not an organization—a spiritual building, not a physical meeting space.

Colossians 1:15-20   **1 Corinthians 12:12-27**
Ephesians 2:19-22   **Romans 12:3-13**

In what ways will you serve the body and be a part of it? How will deep connection to the church build you up in Christ more than going it alone?

Taking Care of Each Part

Even though we are all a part of one body, we all have differences that are to be celebrated. No matter where you are in your life, God's word speaks to your situation in the context of Christian community:

Relationships and Singlehood

1 Corinthians 15:33   Ephesians 5:1-3
1 Corinthians 7:8-9   2 Corinthians 6:14-18

Marriage and Parenting

Ephesians 5:22-6:1-4   1 Peter 3:1-7

Giving/Tithing

Malachi 3:6-10   2 Corinthians 9:7

Questions to Explore

■ Describe what deep commitment to the church will look like. Why is it so important to be committed?

■ How will the church help you grow spiritually? How will you help the church grow?

■ What do you look forward to with regard to a small group discipleship? What are your concerns?

■ Why there is no such thing as a Christian that is not connected to a Christian community (church)?

Next Meet Up with Study Partner _____
Notes:

_____

_____

_____

_____

_____

_____

_____

_____

_____

Counting the Cost
Going All In and All Out for the All In All

"For which of you, desiring to build a tower, does not first sit down and count the cost, whether he has enough to complete it."

— Luke 14:28

A commitment to follow Jesus is the greatest decision we can ever make. It should not be made lightly. How many have sworn allegiance to Jesus during an emotional worship service only to fall away soon after? Jesus asked those who would follow him to count the cost of discipleship. Do you have what it takes to follow him now and forever? May this study give you the confidence and faith you need to make Jesus the Lord of your life.

Luke 9:57-62
- What might keep you from following Jesus?

Mark 4:1-9
- Which soil can you relate to? How will your heart remain good soil for God's word?

Matthew 22:1-14
- Are there any passions keeping you from enjoying God's Kingdom?

Deuteronomy 20:1-9
- Are you focused on God above all?

Review and Discuss:
- Overview of these studies
- Repentance and change
- Walk with God (Reading, Prayer, etc.)
- Biblical conversion
- Relationships and evangelism
- Connecting and giving in the church
- Anticipated challenges and blessings
- Questions

Confirm plans for baptism or membership in the church or discuss more studies.
Finishing this Bible study series and becoming a Christ follower is a big step in your life with God. But it's only the first step! Talk to your Bible study partner about our next

Bible study series that is designed to help you walk with God and discover your place in the church body.

My Ministry _____

My Discipleship Group _____

My first new member study will be: _____
Notes:

_____

_____

_____

_____

_____

_____

_____

_____

_____

_____

Appendix B
Bible Talk Starter Pack

I will host a Bible talk at _____ on _____

I will invite _____

Christians joining me _____

Topic _____

How to Host:

- Set the time and place
- Follow up with the Christians that are coming so they will be there and bring friends
- Ask your friends and neighbors if they will come
- Tidy up the house so that it is an inviting atmosphere
- Provide snacks and refreshments or ask someone in your group to bring some
- Open with an icebreaker question
- Keep it short (20 minutes tops!)
- Focus on only one or two passages (People get insecure if they have to find multiple passages)
- End with a question that leaves people thinking about their heart for God
- Have great conversations afterward about church and/or setting up personal Bible studies
- MAKE IT FUN AND ENGAGING

Four Easy Bible Talks From Jesus' Parables

#1   The Parable of the Sower

Opener: Share your name and ask "Do you have a 'Green Thumb"? Why or why not?"

Introduction: Jesus spoke about agriculture and all kinds of things when he spoke in parables. A parable is a story about everyday life with a deeper spiritual meaning.

Read: Mark 4:1-9
Who do you think the farmer sowing the seed is?
What might the seed be?
And what does the soil represent?
(Hint: It's something that can be different in every person)
When we look at the soils what does each reveal about people's hearts toward the word of God?
Path and Birds -
Rocky Shallow Soil -
Thorns and Weeds -
Good Soil -

This parable is great because we aren't left to figure it out on our own. The disciples didn't understand so they asked Jesus. Here's the explanation from the Word himself—let's see how we did:

Read: Mark 4:13-20
How did we do in our interpretations?

Application

• The most amazing thing about Jesus speaking in parables is that they still apply to our lives 2000 years later.

• Think about your heart toward the word of God? Which soil would you say the word hits? Which soil is the biggest temptation for you?

• What would a heart with good soil look like? What might you produce 30, 60, 100 fold for the kingdom of God?

Close the discussion with a prayer.

#2   The Two Roads

Opener: Give your name and share what is the longest or most exciting road trip you've ever been on?

Introduction: Jesus talked about two roads in his longest and most famous sermon—The Sermon on the Mount—let's look at three passages from that sermon.

Read: Matthew 7:7-8
What does Jesus promise in this passage?

Read Matthew 7:13-14
There are two roads. What is the wide road like? What do you think the wide road looks like today?

What is the narrow road like? What kind of people are on the narrow road?

Tough Question: If you had to pick a road that you are on right now, what would you say? Why? (Reminder, there are only two roads!)
In our first passage Jesus promised "Seek and you will find" but in this passage we learn that "those who find it are few." Why do you think that is?

Read: Matthew 6:33 (explain context first about God meeting our greatest needs)
This passage explains how we are to seek God if we really want to find him.

How should we seek God?
What areas of Godliness should we focus on?
What would your life look like if you were to seek the Kingdom and His Righteousness first?

Apply
Invite to Church (the Kingdom) and to study the Bible (Learn His righteousness)

Close the discussion with a prayer.

#3   A Firm Foundation

Icebreaker: Give everyone some cards and tell them to build the highest card castle that they can. After a few minutes have everyone share their name and how they did with the card castle.

Introduction: It's difficult to build a strong house of cards because there is no foundation. Tonight we're going to look at what the scriptures say about building a strong foundation for your life.

Read: Luke 6:46-49

What's the foundation for a strong life according to Jesus?

Who will be affected by the floods/storms of life?

Can you think of any storms that you are going through right now? Keep them in mind as we look at the next verse.

So hearing the word and doing it is really important!

Read : Luke 14:28-30

Let's apply this to building a relationship with God. Often our spiritual decisions are very emotional but Jesus calls us to count the cost.

What are some costs that you see in becoming a real follower of Jesus?

Is there anything that you might have a hard time completing in your walk with God? Anything you are tempted to give up on?

What do you think it should cost to have the gift of God's salvation? (everything and nothing!)

Read : Luke 14:31-33

Who is the big king?

Who is the little king?

Apply

We are kings/queens of our lives—but God will not rest until we live under his gracious reign.

What are the written terms of peace God has given us? (The Word)

What do you need to surrender so you can say you've given him everything?

Close the discussion with a prayer.

#4   The Great Banquet

Icebreaker: Name your favorite beverage. When you close your eyes what do you think God looks like or is like?

We all have pictures of who God is that are shaped by our experiences in life or church or with people who are Christians or who are supposed to be Christians. One of the things Jesus did was challenge what people thought about God and change the way people saw God. We'll see God in a very different way tonight as we look at one of the stories he told. But first we need to do something together:

Let's pretend we're going to have the most amazing party and we have unlimited resources to make this party awesome. We need to use our imaginations. Ask the group questions and write down the responses:

Who will we invite? How will we invite them? Where will the party be? How long will it last? What kind of entertainment? What kind of food? Etc…

Introduction: Read off the details of the party that you came up with and then explain that Jesus said that the kingdom of heaven would be like a party—a great banquet — and God really does have unlimited resources so let's check it out:

Read Luke 14:15-24

So the image that Jesus gives us about God is that God is a party animal. Have you ever thought about God like that?

Our party sounds pretty awesome but can you imagine the kind of party that God could throw? He has unlimited resources! One way to look at the kingdom of God is that God the king is coming back to throw a wedding banquet for his son. Who is Jesus getting married to? Well, through the cross and resurrection we've been united with Jesus for eternity! The banquet is ready and the invites are sent out but what happens?

Q: What are some of their excuses and what parallels do you see in modern life?

Q: What are some things that keep you from partying with God?

Q: What is God's heart toward people?

Q: What can you start doing so you won't miss out on the great banquet of God?

So many of people's ideas about God are really things they've learned from people. The picture of God that the Bible paints is actually very different from what religious people show us. I want to encourage you to read the Bible for yourself. We have a great set of little Bible studies that actually show what it means to follow the God of the Bible and I'd love to answer a question or talk on a deeper level with any of you any time. But for now, God is a party animal—so let's drink some beverages and have some snacks!

Close with a prayer.

Appendix C

Soul Talk: How is Your Soul Doing?

Let me share two passages with you and then I'll ask you a question that I hope you never forget:

Psalm 23:1-3
Matthew 11:28-30

David sings about how God is his shepherd—but he doesn't just take care of him physically—it's deeper than that—God restores David's soul.

Then in Matthew, the good shepherd tells us that in him we can find rest for our souls.

So here's the big question:

How's your soul doing?

Has anyone ever asked you that before? Have you ever thought about the health of your soul?

In light of these two scriptures it's a good question to ask. How's your soul doing?

Last year, I can't even remember when anymore, I met up with a brother (I remember what we ate but not when it was!) and we had a talk that got deep. My soul was in a bad place. I told my friend how I was praying to overcome negative thoughts and bitterness and temptation that were dogging me. I had been praying and fighting the thoughts but still felt discouraged. What I realized from this talk was that this was more than just emotional discouragement—my soul was not doing well.

Let me ask you another question and you can answer it if you can think of an answer:

Q: What is the soul?

Let these passages shape your view of the soul:

Psalm 42:1

> As the deer pants for flowing streams, so pants my soul for you, O God
> My soul thirsts for the living God. When shall I come and appear before
> God?

Jesus when asked the greatest commandment, quotes Moses in Deuteronomy 4

Matthew 22:37

Love the Lord your God with all your heart and with all your soul and with all your mind.

The apostle John in 3 John, greets his friend like this:
Dear friend, I pray that you may enjoy good health and that all may go well with you, even as your soul is getting along well.

Jesus never speaks lightly of the soul—and yet how often do we even think of it:

Matthew 16:26
For what will it profit a man if he gains the whole world and forfeits his soul? Or what shall a man give in return for his soul?

We focus on being financially healthy but how often do we make sure our souls are healthy?

Matthew 10:28
And do not fear those who kill the body but cannot kill the soul. Rather fear him who can destroy both soul and body in hell.

We focus on keeping our bodies healthy but are we giving our souls the attention they need?

C. S. Lewis defines it without defining it in the most profound way: "You don't have a soul—you are a soul."

Matthew 26:38
My soul is very sorrowful...

When I looked at Jesus' words and then looked at my heart, I realized I was suffering in my soul—if you asked me how my soul was doing I would say very bad - and an alarm went off for me that I can't let myself stay in this place because the enemy wants to kill my soul. Soul sickness leads to death that lasts forever.

How's your soul doing?

Our souls get weary, they get worn out - a lot like the soles of our shoes - you have to get refreshed from time to time.

Q: What are some things that maybe are wearing out your soul?
Here's what I came up with:

Distance from God and his people—God created our souls—Genesis 2 in the KJV says that God breathed life into man and he became a living soul. Your soul will wear out when you are disconnected from the creator of your soul and the savior of your soul.

Emotions and attitudes—our hearts can mess up our soul - that's where I was - if we don't pray to God deep prayers about how we are feeling then we have no way of working out our emotions—we become prisoners to how we feel instead of being in control and having perspective from the creator of our emotions and attitudes.

Social media and information and infotainment—I think it's taking a toll on our souls —when we allow ourselves to be controlled by information instead of using it as a tool we become the tool and our souls suffer for it.

Impurity—Our body is a temple for our souls and for the Holy Spirit and when we let impurity in through our eyes, through our hearts, or through addiction, we are wounding our souls and grieving the Spirit.

Is something hurting your soul?

It's so important to realize that we are more than just flesh and bone and the things that cause us to struggle affect not just our lives but our souls.

So what do we do to restore our souls if they are not doing well?

Knowing is half the battle: recognizing that the most important part of you- your soul - needs attention is a great first step.

Once we start to think on a deeper, eternal level we can really hear Jesus' words in Matthew 11:28-30 and God can restore our souls.

Matthew 11:28-30

We have to get rest for our souls.

And there is a very specific way that we are told to do this:

We don't rest our souls by taking a nap or by taking a vacation or vegging out—that may help our bodies and our minds but—how do we get rest for our souls?

We can only get that from Jesus. We go to Jesus, the good shepherd, and he restores our souls. He gives us rest when we go to him.

Here's what that looked like for me. Obviously I'm in my Bible all the time as a minister, I'm praying, I'm with the church—but I can do all that—we can do all of that and still not be going to Jesus.

Here's how we come to Jesus—through the gospel:

Mark 1:14-15

Jesus came with good news or *gospel*. The news is that now that he's come, God's kingdom has come. If you look at the big picture of our world, you see these movements of God.

First, he created everything including us and his creation was good and very good. But you look at the world and there's a lot of bad and very bad happening. That's on us —we sin, we've fallen from the good we were created to be. We live in self rule instead of trusting our creator's rule. But God wants us to know him and to love him so he sent his son to show us how to live and to die for us so we could be redeemed. Jesus' sacrificial death on the cross bought us back from the death our sin earned. But even though he died and arose some 2000 years ago, we still live in a world full of sin and death. Creation, fall, redemption... the next movement of God is restoration - he's coming back to make everything right—to restore all things including us.

This is why it's so important for us to work on our souls, we don't have to wait for God to come back and restore everything—we can start by going to him and having our souls restored. We can go to Jesus and find rest for our souls even in a fallen world.

That's the good news—the kingdom is here because Jesus is here. His Spirit co-mingles with our souls and brings life.

But we have to repent and believe the good news. REPENT doesn't sound like good news does it? I picture those street preachers yelling about everyone going to hell if they don't repent. Maybe you thought that's what this would be all about tonight. Repent simply means to change your perspective. From your perspective to God's. The kingdom of God is in your midst—will you live in God's kingdom or continue to build your own?

That's repentance. And it's such good news for those who believe that Jesus is Lord!

Coming to Jesus is a changing of allegiances, a changing of nationalities—you are no longer your own—you were bought at a price and now you are God's forever just like you were always supposed to be.

You can't have your soul restored when your living in your own kingdom. You can't come to Jesus and find rest for your soul when you don't accept Jesus' yoke.

Here's what I needed to do: as I thought about my soul—I went into the woods where I always pray—But I prayed differently—I put my soul before God. I brought my soul to Jesus and I surrendered to the true king.

I prayed this: God I can't stop having these negative thoughts. I can't overcome these emotions. My thought life is a mess right now. I am trying to fight all of these thoughts but I cannot do it. I need you God.

I came out of that prayer restored. I have felt like a different person ever since. I truly feel like my soul has been healed. Like it went on vacation and life is easier and lighter now no matter how hard it gets. I'm able to deal with my thought life and I feel Jesus' presence in it all. I have to keep going to Jesus and keep surrendering - and I keep finding rest for my soul.

Jesus has invited each of us to go to him—to admit that we can't restore our souls—we can't save ourselves—to tell him where your soul is at—and receive rest from the only source.

Close

I know you feel it—that there's more to life than the day to day grind. We get weighed down and our souls cry out for something more.

That something more is Jesus Christ and his kingdom—his life.

If you haven't made him the Lord of your life, then I want you to pray with me right now and begin the journey.

[Pray for the souls of the people]

As a church we don't follow the rules or ideas of men—we look for God in his word by studying the Bible. Some next steps for your soul might include prayer, reading the Bible, meeting up for a bible study and coming to church even this Sunday.

Talk with the people you came with and let them know one thing you'll do for your soul because of our time together tonight!

www.HometownMissionary.com

Imagine a church full of Hometown Missionaries! If you've been encouraged by the content of this book let you ministry leader know about hometownmissionary.com. Everything your group needs to make this book a church wide focus is available for free along with coaching. The book can be done in a 12 week period or broken into 3 one month focuses.

Bulk ordering and information about the *Old School Bible Study Series* is available at **KingdomBuiltResources.com**. Similar resources like disciple making studies, new Christian (follow up) studies, and leadership resources are all available in high quality booklet format for the lowest possible price. New resources are added that work for our church as they become available so check back often.

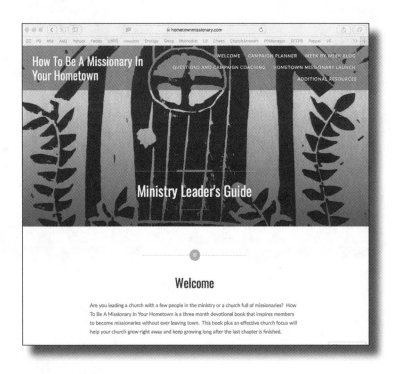

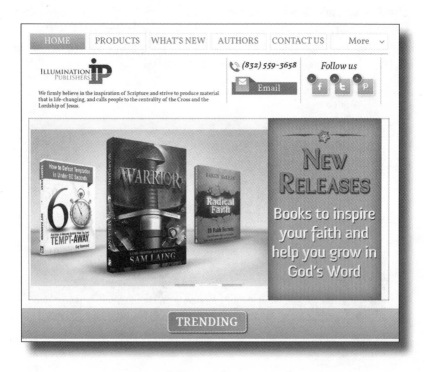

For additional copies of
How to Be a Missionary in Your Hometown
and many other titles, go to
www.ipibooks.com